A Hundred Verses from Old Japan

William N. Porter translated many works from the Japanese between 1900 and 1914. He is best known for his challenging but artful translation of *A Hundred Verses from Old Japan: Being a Translation of the "Hyaku-nin-isshiu"* (1909), a collection of a hundred specimens of Japanese classical *tanka* (poetry written in a five-line 31-syllable format in a 5-7-5-7-7 pattern) dating from the seventh to thirteenth centuries. Another of his well-known translations is *The Tosa Diary*, written in 935 by Ki no Tsurayuki, which is the oldest extant Japanese work of literature.

William N. Porter

A Hundred Verses from Old Japan

Being a translation of the
Hyaku-nin-isshiu

TUTTLE PUBLISHING
Tokyo • Rutland, Vermont • Singapore

Published by Tuttle Publishing, an imprint of Periplus Editions (HK) Ltd,
with editorial offices at 364 Innovation Drive, North Clarendon,
Vermont 05759 and 130 Joo Seng Road #06-01, Singapore 368357

ISBN 13: 978-4-8053-0853-0
ISBN 10: 4-8053-0853-2

Printed in Singapore

Distributed by:

North America, Latin America & Europe
Tuttle Publishing
364 Innovation Drive
North Clarendon, VT 05759-9436 U.S.A.
Tel: 1 (802) 773-8930; Fax: 1 (802) 773-6993
info@tuttlepublishing.com
www.tuttlepublishing.com

Japan
Tuttle Publishing
Yaekari Building, 3rd Floor
5-4-12 Osaki, Shinagawa-ku
Tokyo 141 0032
Tel: (81) 03 5437-0171; Fax: (81) 03 5437-0755
tuttle-sales@gol.com

Asia Pacific
Berkeley Books Pte. Ltd.
130 Joo Seng Road #06-01
Singapore 368357
Tel: (65) 6280-1330; Fax: (65) 6280-6290
inquiries@periplus.com.sg
www.periplus.com

07 09 11 12 10 08
1 3 5 6 4 2

TUTTLE PUBLISHING® is a registered trademark of Tuttle Publishing,
a division of Periplus Editions (HK) Ltd.

PUBLISHER'S FOREWORD

This early translation of one of Japan's most celebrated anthologies of poetry has preserved its charm for almost seventy years, and it is a distinct satisfaction to make it available once more for the pleasure of discerning readers. First published in 1909 and unjustly out of print for far too long a time, it makes a new appearance here for the enjoyment of all who appreciate writing of a truly engaging quality. Mr. Porter's translation is truly a labor of love, and the fact that several other English translations of the work have appeared in later years in no way diminishes the value of his accomplishment.

The *Hyakunin Isshu* (or *Isshiu,* as Mr. Porter transliterates the word) dates from the thirteenth century and is by far the most popular of classical poetry anthologies among the Japanese. The collection consists almost entirely of love poems and picture poems intended to bring some well-known scene to mind. As Mr. Porter points out, it is astonishing "what perfect little thumbnail sketches are compressed within thirty-one syllables." The long-standing love of the Japanese for this evocative and intensely human poetry is reflected in the translation, and the publisher takes more than the usual amount of pleasure in bringing Mr. Porter's book once more to light.

INTRODUCTION

THE *Hyaku-nin-isshiu, or* 'Single Verses by a Hundred People', were collected together in A.D. 1235 by Sadaiye Fujiwara, who included as his own contribution verse No. 97. They are placed in approximately chronological order, and range from about the year 670 to the year of compilation. The Japanese devote themselves to poetry very much more than we do; and there is hardly a home in Japan, however humble, where these verses, or at least some of them, are not known. They are, and have been for many years, used also in connection with a game of cards, in which the skill consists in fitting parts of the different verses together.

Japanese poetry differs very largely from anything we are used to; it has no rhyme or alliteration, and little, if any, rhythm, as we understand it. The verses in this Collection are all what are called *Tanka,* which was for many years the only form of verse known to the Japanese. A *tanka* verse has five lines and thirty-one syllables, arranged thus: 5–7–5–7–7; as this is an unusual meter in our ears, I have adopted for the translation a five-lined verse of 8–6–8–6–6 meter, with the second, fourth, and fifth lines rhyming, in the hope of retaining at least some resemblance to the original form, while making the sound more familiar to English readers.

I may perhaps insert here, as an example, the following well-known *tanka* verse, which does not appear in the *Hyaku-nin-isshiu* collection:—

Idete inaba
Nushinaki yado to
Narinu tomo
Nokiba no ume yo
Haru wo wasuruna.

Though masterless my home appear,
When I have gone away,
Oh plum tree growing by the eaves,
Forget not to display
Thy buds in spring, I pray.

This was written by Sanetomo Minamoto on the morning of the day he was murdered at Kamakura, as related in the note to verse No. 93.

It is necessarily impossible in a translation of this kind to adhere at all literally to the text; more especially as Japanese poetry abounds in all sorts of puns, plays upon words, and alternative meanings, which cannot be rendered into English. For example, a favorite device with Japanese verse-writers is to introduce what Professor Chamberlain calls a 'pivotword', which they consider adds an elegant touch to the composition. An instance of this will be found in verse No. 16, where the word *matsu,* though only appearing once, must be understood twice with its two different meanings. It is almost as if we should say, 'Sympathy is what I *need*less to say I never get it.' Other peculiarities of Japanese verse, as Professor Chamberlain points out, are the 'pillow-word', or recognized conventional epithet (see verse No. 17), and the 'preface', where the first two or three lines appear to have only the slightest connection with the main idea, and simply serve as an introduction (see verse No. 27).

The *Hyaku-nin-isshiu,* like all Japanese classical poetry, contains no Chinese words, such as are so extensively introduced into the modern spoken language; it consists of poetical ideas clothed in poetical language, compressed within the regulation meter, embellished with various elegant word-plays, and is absolutely free from any trace of vulgarity. In the old days it was only the nobles, court officials, and church dignitaries, who wrote verses; or at all events only their verses have been handed down to our time, and the lower classes were not supposed to know anything at all about the art.

Thus, it is related that long ago Prince Ota Dokwan was hunting with his retinue on the mountains; and, a storm of rain coming on, he stopped at a mountain inn, to request the loan of a rain-coat; a girl came at his call, and retired into the hut, coming back again in a few minutes looking rather confused, and without saying a word she humbly presented the Prince with a yamabuki blossom (a kind of yellow rose) on an outstretched fan. The Prince, much incensed at being trifled with like this, turned on his heel, and went off in high dudgeon; until one of his attendants reminded him of a well-known verse, which runs:—

> Nanae yae
> Hana wa sake domo
> Yamabuki no
> Mi no hitotsu dani
> Naki zo kanashiki.

> The yamabuki blossom has
> A wealth of petals gay;
> But yet in spite of this, alas!
> I much regret to say,
> No seed can it display.

The words as printed in the last couplet mean, 'I am very sorry that it has not a single seed'; but, if *mino* is taken as one word, it would mean, 'I am very sorry that (the yamabuki, i.e. herself, the mountain flower) has not any rain-coat'. And this was the maiden's delicate apology. The Prince, we are told, was astonished to find such culture and learning in a peasant girl!

Perhaps what strikes one most in connection with the *Hyaku-nin-isshiu* is the date when the verses were written; most of them were produced before the time of the Norman Conquest, and one cannot but be struck with the advanced state of art and culture in Japan at a time when England was still in a very elementary stage of civilization.

The Collection, as will be seen, consists almost entirely of love-poems and what I may call picture-poems, intended to bring before the mind's eye some well-known scene in nature; and it is marvellous what perfect little thumbnail sketches are compressed within thirty-one syllables, however crude and faulty the translation may be; for instance, verses Nos. 79, 87, and 98. But the predominating feature, the undercurrent that runs through them all, is a touch of pathos, which is characteristic of the Japanese. It shows out in the cherry blossoms which are doomed to fall, the dewdrops scattered by the wind, the mournful cry of the wild deer on the mountains, the dying crimson of the fallen maple leaves, the weird sadness of the cuckoo singing in the moonlight, and the loneliness of the recluse in the mountain wilds; while those verses which appear to be of a more cheerful type are rather of the nature of the 'Japanese smile', described by Lafcadio Hearn as a mask to hide the real feelings.

Some explanation is necessary as to the names of the writers of the different verses. The Japanese custom is to place the family or clan name first, followed by the preposition *no* (of), and then the rest of the name; but, as this would be appreciated only by those who are familiar with the language, the names have been transposed, and the titles ranks translated, as far as possible, into English. At the same time the full name and title have also been given on the left hand page in their Japanese form; for many of these names, such as Yamabe no Akahito, Abe no Nakamaro, Ono no Komachi, are so well known to Japanese students that they would hardly be recognized in their transposed form.

A word may be added as to pronounciation, for the benefit of those who are not familiar with Japanese; every vowel in poetry must be sounded, there are no diphthongs, a long vowel is lengthened out, as if it were two syllables, a final *n*, which was originally *mu*, must be sounded as a full syllable, and a final vowel is generally elided, if the following word begins with a vowel. The continental sound is to be given to *a*, *e*, and *i*, and the aspirate is sounded.

The illustrations have been reproduced from a native edition of the *Hyaku-nin-isshiu,* which probably dates from the end of the eighteenth century, and which has been kindly lent to me by Mr. F. V. Dickins, C.B., to whom I am much indebted; as will be seen, they generally illustrate the subject of the verse, but occasionally they appear to represent the conditions under which the verse was written.

For most of the information contained in the notes the present Translator is indebted to the researches of Professor B. H. Chamberlain, F.R.G.S., Professor Clay MacCauley, and Mr. F.V. Dickins, C.B.; his thanks are also due to Mr. S.

Uchigasaki, for his kind assistance towards the meaning of some of the more obscure passages. He makes no claim that his verses have any merit as English poetry; nor, where there is so much uncertainty among the Japanese themselves as to the real meaning of some of these old verses, does he claim that his translation is in all cases the correct one. In two or three instances the original has been purposely toned down somewhat, to suit English ideas. He has, however, tried to reproduce these Verses from Old Japan in such a way, that a few of the many, who now are unfamiliar with the subject, may feel sufficient interest in them to study a more scholarly translation, such as that by Mr. F. V. Dickins, published in the *Journal of the Royal Asiatic Society*, or Professor MacCauley's literal translation, both of which are evidently the result of hard labor and great care; and may thus learn to appreciate a branch of Japanese art which has been far too much neglected up to the present.

W. N. P.

'Whatever Defects, as, I doubt not, there will be many, fall under the Reader's Observation, I hope his Candour will incline him to make the following Reflections: That the Works of *Orientals* contain many Peculiarities, and that thro' Defect of Language few *European* Translators can do them Justice.'

WILLIAM COLLINS.

TENJI TENNŌ

Aki no ta no
Kari ho no iho no
Toma wo arami
Waga koromode wa
Tsuyu ni nure-tsutsu.

天智天皇

秋の田のかりほの庵の苫をあらみ

わが衣手は露にぬれつつ

THE EMPEROR TENJI

OUT in the fields this autumn day
  They're busy reaping grain;
I sought for shelter 'neath this roof,
  But fear I sought in vain,—
  My sleeve is wet with rain.

The Emperor Tenji reigned from A.D. 668 to 671, his capital was Otsu, not far from Kyōto, and he is chiefly remembered for his kindness and benevolence. It is related, that one day he was scaring birds away, while the harvesters were gathering in the crop, and, when a shower of rain came on, he took shelter in a neighboring hut; it was, however, thatched only with coarse rushes, which did not afford him much protection, and this is the incident on which the verse is founded.

The picture shows the harvesters hard at work in the field, and the hut where the Emperor took shelter.

JITŌ TENNŌ

Haru sugite
Natsu ki ni kerashi
Shirotae no
Koromo hosu teu
Ama-no-kagu yama

持統天皇

春すぎて夏来にけらし白妙の

衣ほすてふ天の香具山

THE EMPRESS JITŌ

THE spring has gone, the summer's come,
   And I can just descry
The peak of Ama-no-kagu,
   Where angels of the sky
   Spread their white robes to dry.

The Empress Jitō reigned A.D. 690–696, during which time saké was first made and drunk in Japan; she was the daughter of the Emperor Tenji, the writer of the previous verse, and she married the Emperor Temmu, ascending the throne herself on his death. The poem refers to a snow-capped mountain just visible on the horizon. One of the Nō dramas relates, that an angel once came to a pine forest on the coast near Okitsu, and, hanging her feather mantle on a pine tree, climbed a neighboring mountain to view Mount Fuji; a fisherman, however, found the robe and was about to carry it off with him, when the angel reappeared and begged him to give it her, as without it she could not return to the moon where she lived. He only consented to do so, however, on condition that she would dance for him; and this she accordingly did, draped in her feathery robe on the sandy beach under the shade of the pine trees; after which she floated heavenward, and was lost to view.

KAKI-NO-MOTO NO HITOMARO

Ashibiki no
Yamadori no o no
Shidario no
Naga-nagashi yo wo
Hitori ka mo nemu.

柿本人麻呂

あしびきの山鳥の尾のしだり尾の

ながながし夜を独かもねむ

THE NOBLEMAN KAKI-NO-MOTO

LONG is the mountain pheasant's tail
That curves down in its flight;
But longer still, it seems to me,
Left in my lonely plight,
Is this unending night.

The writer was a foundling, picked up and adopted by
Abaye at the foot of a persimmon tree, which is in Japanese
kaki, from which he got his name. He was an attendant on the
Emperor Mommu, who reigned A.D. 697–707, and was one of
the great poets of the early days of Japan; he is known as the
rival of Akahito Yamabe (see next verse), and after death was
deified as a God of Poetry. There is a temple erected in his
honor at Ichi-no-Moto, and another at Akashi, not far from
Kobe; he died in the year 737.

In the fourth line *nagashi* may be taken as the adjective
'long', or the verb 'to drift along'; and *yo* may mean either
'night' or 'life'; so that this line, which I have taken as 'long,
long is the night', may also mean 'my life is drifting, drifting
along'. *Yamadori* (pheasant) is literally 'mountain bird', and
ashibiki is a pillow-word for mountain, which is itself the first
half of the word for pheasant.

YAMABE NO AKAHITO

Tago no ura ni
Uchi-idete mireba
Shirotae no
Fuji no takane ni
Yuki wa furi-tsutsu.

やまべのあかひと
山辺赤人

た　ご　うら　　　　　い　　　　　　　　　しろたへ
田子の浦にうち出でてみれば白妙の

ふじ　たかね　　　　　　　　　ふ
不二の高根にゆきは降りつつ

AKAHITO YAMABE

I STARTED off along the shore,
　The sea shore at Tago,
And saw the white and glist'ning peak
　Of Fuji all aglow
　Through falling flakes of snow.

Akahito Yamabe lived about A.D. 700, and was one of the greatest of the early poets; he was contemporary with Kaki-no-Moto, the writer of the previous verse, and like him was deified as a God of Poetry. Tago is a seaside place in the Province of Izu, famous for its beautiful view of Mount Fuji.

SARU MARU DAYŪ

Oku yama ni
Momiji fumi wake
Naku shika no
Koe kiku toki zo
Aki wa kanashiki.

猿丸大夫

おく山に紅葉ふみわけ鳴く鹿の

聲きくときぞ秋はかなしき

SARU MARU, A SHINTO OFFICIAL

I HEAR the stag's pathetic call
   Far up the mountain side,
While tramping o'er the maple leaves
   Wind-scattered far and wide
   This sad, sad autumn tide.

Very little is known of this writer, but he probably lived not later than A.D. 800. Stags and the crimson leaves of the maple are frequently used symbolically of autumn.

CHŪ-NAGON YAKAMOCHI

Kasasagi no
Wataseru hashi ni
Oku shimo no
Shiroki wo mireba
Yo zo fuke ni keru.

ちゅうなごん やか もち
中納言家持

かささぎ わた　　　　　　　　　　しも
鵲の渡せるはしにおく霜の

　　　　　　　　　　　よ　　ふけ
しろきをみれば夜ぞ更にける

THE IMPERIAL ADVISER YAKAMOCHI

WHEN on the Magpies' Bridge I see
The Hoar-frost King has cast
His sparkling mantle, well I know
The night is nearly past,
Daylight approaches fast

The author of this verse was Governor of the Province of Kōshū, and Viceroy of the more or less uncivilized northern and eastern parts of Japan; he died A.D. 785. There was a bridge or passageway in the Imperial Palace at Kyōto called the Magpies' Bridge, but there is also an allusion here to the old legend about the Weaver and Herdsman. It is said, that the Weaver (the star Vega) was a maiden, who dwelt on one side of the River of the Milky Way, and who was employed in making clothes for the Gods. But one day the Sun took pity upon her, and gave her in marriage to the Herdboy (the star Aquila), who lived on the other side of the river. But as the result of this was that the supply of clothes fell short, she was only permitted to visit her husband once a year, viz. on the seventh night of the seventh month; and on this night, it is said, the magpies in a dense flock form a bridge for her across the river. The hoar frost forms just before day breaks. The illustration shows the Herdboy crossing on the Bridge of Magpies to his bride.

ABE NO NAKAMARO

Ama no hara
Furisake-mireba
Kasuga naru
Mikasa no yama ni
Ideshi tsuki kamo.

安倍仲麿

天の原ふりさけみれば春日なる

三笠の山に出でし月かも

NAKAMARO ABE

WHILE gazing up into the sky,
  My thoughts have wandered far;
Methinks I see the rising moon
  Above Mount Mikasa
  At far-off Kasuga.

The poet, when sixteen years of age, was sent with two others to China, to discover the secret of the Chinese calendar, and on the night before sailing for home his friends gave him a farewell banquet. It was a beautiful moonlight night, and after dinner he composed this verse. Another account, however, says that the Emperor of China, becoming suspicious, caused him to be invited to a dinner at the top of a high pagoda, and then had the stairs removed, in order that he might be left to die of hunger. Nakamaro is said to have bitten his hand and written this verse with his blood, after which he appears to have escaped and fled to Annam. Kasuga, pronounced Kasunga, is a famous temple at the foot of Mount Mikasa, near Nara, the poet's home; the verse was written in the year 726, and the author died in 780.

KISEN HŌSHI

Waga iho wa
Miyako no tatsumi
Shika zo sumu
Yo wo Uji yama to
Hito wa iu nari.

喜撰法師

わが庵は都のたつみしかぞすむ

世をうぢ山とひとはいふなり

THE PRIEST KISEN

MY home is near the Capital,
  My humble cottage bare
Lies south-east on Mount Uji; so
  The people all declare
  My life's a 'Hill of Care'.

The priest Kisen lived on Mount Uji, which lies south-east of Kyōto, at this time the Capital. The word *uji* or *ushi* means 'sorrow'; so he says that, as he lives on Mount Sorrow, his friends say his life is 'a mountain of sorrows'. Notice also the two words *yama to* in the fourth line, which, if read as one word, form the ancient name of Japan. In the picture we see the priest sitting alone in his little hut, his poverty being shown by the patches on the roof.

ONO NO KOMACHI

Hana no iro wa
Utsuri ni keri na
Itazura ni
Waga mi yo ni furu
Nagame seshi ma ni.

小野小町

花の色はうつりにけりないたづらに

わが身世にふるながめせしまに

KOMACHI ONO

THE blossom's tint is washed away
  By heavy showers of rain;
My charms, which once I prized so much,
  Are also on the wane,—
  Both bloomed, alas! in vain.

The writer was a famous poetess, who lived A.D. 834–880. She is remembered for her talent, her beauty, her pride, her love of luxury, her frailty, and her miserable old age. The magic of her art is said to have overcome a severe drought, from which the country suffered in the year 866, when prayers to the Gods had proved useless.

The first and last couplets may mean either 'the blossom's tint fades away under the continued downpour of rain in the world', or 'the beauty of this flower (i.e. herself) is fading away as I grow older and older in this life'; while the third line dividing the two couplets means, that the flower's tint and her own beauty are alike only vanity. This verse, with its double meaning running throughout, is an excellent example of the characteristic Japanese play upon words.

SEMI MARU

Kore ya kono
Yuku mo kaeru mo
Wakarete wa
Shiru mo shiranu mo
Ausaka no seki.

蝉丸

これやこの行も帰るもわかれては

しるもしらぬも逢坂の関

SEMI MARU

THE stranger who has traveled far,
The friend with welcome smile,
All sorts of men who come and go
Meet at this mountain stile,—
They meet and rest awhile.

Semi Maru is said to have been the son of the Emperor Uda, who reigned A.D. 888–897. He became blind, and so, being unable to ascend the throne, he retired to a hut on the hills, near to a barrier gate, and amused himself with his guitar. The translation does not fully reproduce the antithesis of the original— 'this or that man, people coming and going, long lost friends and strangers'. The last line is literally 'the barrier on the mountain road of meeting'; and Ōsaka no Seki, as the name is now spelled, a small hill on the edge of Lake Biwa, not far from Kyōto, is the site commemorated in this verse.

SANGI TAKAMURA

Wata no hara
Yasoshima kakete
Kogi idenu to
Hito ni wa tsugeyo
Ama no tsuribune.

参議篁

わたの原八十島かけて漕ぎ出でぬと
人には告げよ海人のつり舟

THE PRIVY COUNCILLOR TAKAMURA

OH! Fishers in your little boats,
Quick! tell my men, I pray,
They'll find me at Yasoshima,
I'm being rowed away
Far off across the bay.

Takamura, a well-known scholar, rose from poverty to riches on being appointed a Custom-house officer for the ships trading to and from China. His enemies reported him to the Emperor as an extortioner and a thief, and he was deported to Yasoshima, a group of small islands off the coast; he is said to have composed this song and sung it to the fishing-boats, as he was being carried off. He was afterwards pardoned and reinstated, dying in the year 852.

SŌJŌ HENJŌ

Amatsu kaze
Kumo no kayoiji
Fuki tojiyo
Otome no sugata
Shibashi todomemu.

そうじょうへんじょう
僧正遍昭

あま　かぜ　くも　　　　　　　　ち　ふ
天つ風雲のかよひ路吹きとぢよ

すがた
をとめの姿しばしとどめむ

BISHOP HENJŌ

OH stormy winds, bring up the clouds,
  And paint the heavens grey;
Lest these fair maids of form divine
  Should angel wings display,
  And fly far far away.

The poet's real name was Munesada Yoshimune, and he
was the great-grandson of the Emperor Kwammu. On the death
of the Emperor Nimmyō, to whom he was much devoted (A.D.
850), he took holy orders, and in the year 866 was made a bi-
shop. He died in the year 890, at the age of seventy, from being
buried, by his own wish, in a small stone tomb covered with
soil, with only a small pipe leading from his mouth to the open
air; he remained thus, until hunger and exhaustion put an end
to his life. He is said to have composed the above verse, before
he entered the priesthood, on seeing a dance of some maidens
at a Court entertainment; he pretends that the ladies are so
beautiful that they can be nothing less than angels, and he is
afraid they will fly away, unless the wind will bring up the
clouds to bar their passage. In the picture he is shown with two
acolytes, apparently addressing the wind.

YŌZEI IN

Tsukuba ne no
Mine yori otsuru
Mina no gawa
Koi zo tsumorite
Fuchi to nari nuru.

ようぜいいん
陽成院

つくば ね　　　　　　　　お　　　　　がは
筑波嶺のみねより落つるみなの川

こひ　　　　　　　　ふち
恋ぞつもりて淵となりぬる

THE RETIRED EMPEROR YŌZEI

THE Mina stream comes tumbling down
  From Mount Tsukuba's height;
Strong as my love, it leaps into
  A pool as black as night
  With overwhelming might.

It was a frequent custom in the old days for the Emperors of Japan to retire into the church or private life, when circumstances demanded it. The Emperor Yōzei, who was only nine years of age when he came to the throne, went out of his mind, and was forced by Mototsune Fujiwara to retire; he reigned A.D. 877–884, and did not die till the year 949. The verse was addressed to the Princess Tsuridono-no-Miko. Mount Tsukuba (2,925 feet high) and the River Mina are in the Province of Hitachi.

Koi here means the dark color of the water from its depth, but it also means his love, and is to be understood both ways. Note also *mine*, a mountain peak, and *Mina*, the name of the river.

KAWARA NO SADAIJIN

Michinoku no
Shinobu moji-zuri
Tare yue ni
Midare-some nishi
Ware naranaku ni.

河原左大臣

みちのくのしのぶもぢずりたれ故に

乱れそめにしわれならなくに

THE MINISTER-OF-THE-LEFT OF THE KAWARA (DISTRICT OF KYŌTO)

AH! why does love distract my thoughts,
  Disordering my will!
I'm like the pattern on the cloth
  Of Michinoku hill,—
  All in confusion still.

The old capital of Kyōto was divided into right and left districts, and the above is only an official title; the poet's name was Tōru Minamoto, and he died in the year 949. At Michinoku, in the Province of Iwashiro, in old times a kind of figured silk fabric was made, called *moji-zuri,* embroidered with an intricate pattern, which was formed by placing vine leaves on the material, and rubbing or beating them with a stone until the impression was left on the silk. There is a hill close by, called Mount Shinobu, and a small temple, called Shinobu Moji-zuri Kwannon. *Shinobu* can also mean 'a vine', 'to love', or to 'conceal (my love)'. The meaning of this very involved verse appears to be, that his thoughts are as confused with love as the vine pattern on the embroidered fabric made at Mount Michinoku. The picture seems to show the lady with whom the poet was in love.

KWŌKŌ TENNŌ

Kimi ga tame
Haru no no ni idete
Wakana tsumu
Waga koromode ni
Yuki wa furi-tsutsu.

こうこうてんのう
光孝天皇

きみ　　　　　はる　の　　　い　　　　　わかな
君がため春の野に出でて若菜つむ

ころもで　　ゆき　ふ
わが衣手に雪は降りつつ

THE EMPEROR KWŌKŌ

MOTHER, for thy sake I have been
  Where the wakana grow,
To bring thee back some fresh green leaves;
  And see—my koromo
  Is sprinkled with the snow!

Kwōkō was raised to the throne by the Fujiwara family, when the mad Emperor Yōzei was deposed; he reigned A.D. 885–887, and is said to have composed this verse in honor of his grandmother.

Wakana, literally 'young leaves', is a vegetable in season at the New Year; a *koromo* is really a priest's garment, but is used here for the Emperor's robe.

In the picture we see the Emperor gathering the fresh green leaves, and the snow falling from the sky.

CHŪ-NAGON YUKIHIRA

Tachi wakare
Inaba no yama no
Mine ni ouru
Matsu to shi kikaba
Ima kaeri-komu.

ちゅうなごんゆきひら
中納言行平

たち別れいなばの山の峰に生ふる

まつとし聞かばいま帰りこむ

THE IMPERIAL ADVISER YUKIHIRA

IF breezes on Inaba's peak
　　Sigh through the old pine tree,
To whisper in my lonely ears
　　That thou dost pine for me,—
　　Swiftly I'll fly to thee.

Yukihira Ariwara was the Governor of the Province of Inaba, and half-brother of the writer of the next verse; he died in the year 893, aged 75.

The word *matsu* in the original may mean 'a pine tree', but it may also mean 'waiting and longing for'. This is an instance of a 'pivot-word', imitated to a certain extent in the translation, although in English we have to employ the word twice over, while it only appears once in the Japanese.

The illustration shows the pine tree on the mountain, and the poet standing under it with two attendants.

ARIWARA NO NARIHIRA ASON

Chi haya buru
Kami yo mo kikazu
Tatsuta gawa
Kara kurenai ni
Mizu kukuru to wa.

在原業平朝臣

ちはやぶる神代もきかず竜田川

からくれなゐに水くくるとは

THE MINISTER NARIHIRA ARIWARA

ALL red with leaves Tatsuta's stream
    So softly purls along,
The everlasting Gods themselves,
    Who judge 'twixt right and wrong,
    Ne'er heard so sweet a song.

The writer, who lived A.D. 825–880, was the grandson of the Emperor Saga, and was the Don Juan of Old Japan; he was banished because of an intrigue he had with the Empress, and his adventures are fully related in the Ise-Monogatari. The Tatsuta stream is not far from Nara, and is famous for its maples in autumn. *Chi haya furu*, literally 'thousand quick brandishing (swords)', is a 'pillow-word', or recognized epithet, for the Gods, and almost corresponds to Virgil's *Pious Aeneas*, and Homer's '*Odysseus, the son of Zeus, Odysseus of many devices*'. It may be noted that these 'pillow-words' only occur in the five-syllable lines, never in the longer lines.

In the picture we see the poet looking at a screen, on which is depicted the river with the red maple leaves floating on it.

FUJIWARA NO TOSHIYUKI ASON

Sumi-no-ye no
Kishi ni yoru nami
Yoru sae ya
Yume no kayoi-ji
Hito-me yokuramu.

藤原敏行朝臣

住の江の岸に寄る波よるさへや

夢の通ひ路人目よくらむ

THE MINISTER TOSHIYUKI FUJIWARA

TO-NIGHT on Sumi-no-ye beach
The waves alone draw near;
And, as we wander by the cliffs,
No prying eyes shall peer,
No one shall dream we're here.

Toshiyuki, who lived A.D. 880–907, was an officer of the Imperial Guard, and a member of the great and influential Fujiwara family. This family rose into power in the reign of the Emperor Tenji, and became almost hereditary ministers-of-state. For a long period the Emperors chose their wives from this family only, and to this day a large number of the Japanese nobility are sprung from the same stock. Sumi-no-ye, or Sumi-yoshi, is in the Province of Settsu, near Kobe.

Note the word *yoru* used twice; in the first instance as a verb, meaning 'to approach', and in the next line meaning 'night'. The illustration shows Toshiyuki walking on the beach, and evidently waiting for the lady to join him.

ISE

Naniwa gata
Mijikaki ashi no
Fushi no ma mo
Awade kono yo wo
Sugushite yo to ya.

伊勢

難波潟みじかき芦のふしの間も
逢はでこの世をすぐしてよとや

THE PRINCESS ISE

SHORT as the joints of bamboo reeds
 That grow beside the sea
On pebble beach at Naniwa,
 I hope the time may be,
 When thou'rt away from me.

The Princess Ise was the daughter of Tsugukage Fujiwara, the Governor of the Province of Ise; hence her name. She lived at the Imperial Court, and was the favorite maid of honor of the Emperor Uda, who reigned A.D. 888–897. She was noted for her talents and gentle disposition, and was the mother of Prince Katsura. Naniwa is the old name of Ōsaka. The picture shows the Princess on the pebble beach at Naniwa, and to the left are the bamboo reeds.

MOTOYOSHI SHINNŌ

Wabi nureba
Ima hata onaji
Naniwa naru
Mi wo tsukushite mo
Awamu to zo omou.

元良親王

わびぬれば今はたおなじ難波なる

みをつくしても逢はむとぞ思ふ

THE HEIR-APPARENT MOTOYOSHI

WE met but for a moment, and
  I'm wretched as before;
The *tide* shall *measure* out my life,
  Unless I see once more
  The maid, whom I adore.

The composer of this verse was the son of the Emperor Yōzei, who reigned A.D. 877–884; he was noted for his love-affairs, and he died in the year 943.

Mi wo tsukushite mo means 'even though I die in the attempt', but *miotsukushi* is a graduated stick, set up to measure the rise and fall of the tide; and Naniwa, the modern seaport of Ōsaka, seems to have been inserted chiefly as the place where this tide-gauge was set up. The poet may have meant, that the river of his tears was so deep as to require a gauge to measure it; or, as Professor MacCauley reads it, he was hinting, that if he could not attain his ends his body would be found at the tide-gauge in Naniwa Bay. The picture seems to show the poet on the verandah and his lady-love looking through the screen.

SOSEI HŌSHI

Ima komu to
Iishi bakari ni
Naga-tsuki no
Ariake no tsuki wo
Machi idetsuru kana.

素性法師

いま来こむと言ひしばかりに長月の
有明の月を待ちいでつるかな

THE PRIEST SOSEI

THE moon that shone the whole night through
  This autumn morn I see,
As here I wait thy well-known step,
  For thou didst promise me—
  'I'll surely come to thee.'

Sosei is supposed to have been the son of Bishop Henjō, the
writer of verse No. 12, born before the latter entered the
church, about the year 850. His name as a layman was Hiro-
nobu Yoshimine, and he became abbot of the Monastery of
Riyau-inwin at Iso-no-kami, in the Province of Yamato.

FUNYA NO YASUHIDE

Fuku kara ni
Aki no kusa ki no
Shiorureba
Mube yama kaze wo
Arashi to iuramu.

文屋康秀

吹からに秋の草木のしをるれば
むべ山風を嵐といふらむ

YASUHIDE FUNYA

THE mountain wind in autumn time
  Is well called 'hurricane';
It *hurries canes* and twigs along,
  And whirls them o'er the plain
  To scatter them again.

This well-known writer lived in the ninth century, and was the father of Asayasu, who composed verse No. 37; he was also Vice-Director of the Imperial Bureau of Fabrics.

The point of this verse lies in the ideographic characters of the original; *yama kaze* (mountain wind) being written with two characters, which, when combined, form *arashi* (hurricane), and this, of course, it is quite impossible to reproduce correctly in the translation. The picture shows the wind blowing down from the mountain behind the poet and waving his sleeves about.

ŌYE NO CHISATO

Tsuki mireba
Chiji ni mono koso
Kanashi kere
Waga mi hitotsu no
Aki ni wa aranedo.

おおえのちさと
大江千里

つきみ　　　　　　　　　　　　　　かな
月見ればちぢにものこそ悲しEKれ

み ひと　　　　　あき
わが身一つの秋にはあらねど

CHISATO ŌYE

THIS night the cheerless autumn moon
   Doth all my mind enthrall;
But others also have their griefs,
   For autumn on us all
   Hath cast her gloomy pall.

Chisato Ōye is said to have lived about the end of the ninth century; he was the son of a Councillor, and a very fertile poet. He was also famous as a philosopher, and acted as tutor to the Emperor Seiwa, who reigned A.D. 859–876.

KWAN-KE

Kono tabi wa
Nusa mo tori-aezu
Tamuke-yama
Momiji no nishiki
Kami no mani-mani.

菅家

このたびは幣もとりあへず手向山

紅葉の錦神のまにまに

KWAN-KE

I BRING no prayers on colored silk
  To deck thy shrine to-day,
But take instead these maple leaves,
  That grow at Tamuké;
  Finer than silk are they.

The name given above means 'A house of rushes', but the poet's real name was Michizane Sugawara; he was a great minister in the Emperor Uda's reign and a learned scholar; his works comprise twelve books of poetry and two hundred volumes of history; he was degraded in A.D. 901, and died two years later, an exile in Kyūshū, aged fifty-nine. He is worshipped as Tenjin Sama, the God of Calligraphy, and is a favorite deity with schoolboys.

Nusa are strips of colored silk or cloth inscribed with prayers, which were presented at temples in the old days. Tamuke-yama no Hachiman, a temple at Nara, is the scene of this verse; it is famous for its maple leaves, and the poet intended to say, that the crimson color of its own maples was finer than any brocade that he could offer. Another allusion is, that *Tamuke-yama,* near Nara, means 'The Hill of Offerings'.

SANJŌ NO UDAIJIN

Na ni shi owaba
Ausaka yama no
Sanekazura
Hito ni shirarede
Kuru yoshi mo gana.

さんじょうのうだいじん
三条右大臣

な　　お　　あふさかやま
名にし負はば逢坂山のさねかづら
ひと　し　　く
人に知られで来るよしもがな

THE MINISTER-OF-THE-RIGHT OF THE SANJŌ (DISTRICT OF KYŌTO)

I HEAR thou art as modest as
The little creeping spray
Upon Mount Ōsaka, which hides
Beneath the grass; then, pray,
Wander with me to-day.

The writer's real name was Sadakata Fujiwara, and he died
A.D. 932. For an account of the Fujiwara family see verse No.
18. Mount Ōsaka mentioned here is the same place as that
referred to in verse No. 10, and when spelled *Ausaka* it means
'a hill of meeting'. The suggestion is, that if she is really like
the creeping vine which grows on Meeting Hill, she will come
and meet him.

TEISHIN KŌ

Ogura yama
Mine no momiji-ba
Kokoro araba
Ima hito tabi no
Miyuki matanamu.

<ruby>貞信公<rt>ていしんこう</rt></ruby>

小倉山峰のもみぢ葉こころあらば

今ひとたびのみゆき待たなむ

PRINCE TEISHIN

THE maples of Mount Ogura,
  If they could understand,
Would keep their brilliant leaves, until
  The Ruler of this land
  Pass with his royal band.

The above is the posthumous name given to Tadahira Fujiwara, Imperial Chief Minister of State; he died about the year 936. It is related that the Emperor Uda, after his abdication, visited Mount Ogura in Yamashiro province, and was so greatly struck with the autumn tints of the maples, that he ordered Tadahira to invite his son, the Emperor Daigo, to visit the scene; and this verse was the invitation. The picture shows the Emperor with his attendants, and the maples all around him.

CHŪ-NAGON KANESUKE

Mika no hara
Wakite nagaruru
Izumi gawa
Itsu miki tote ka
Koishi-karuramu.

ちゅうなごんかねすけ
中納言兼輔

みかの原わきて流るるいづみ川

いつみきとてか恋しかるらむ

THE IMPERIAL ADVISER KANESUKE

OH! rippling River Izumi,
  That flows through Mika plain,
Why should the maid I saw but now
  And soon shall see again
  Torment my love-sick brain?

Kanesuke was a member of the Fujiwara family; he died in the year 933. The River Izumi is in the Province of Yamashiro.

The word-plays in this verse are—*Izumi*, in the third line, which is imitated in the next line, and *Mika*, which is also repeated in the third line. The first three lines of this verse, about the river flowing through the plain, form a 'preface', and appear to be inserted merely because *itsu miki* (when I have seen her) sounds like *Izumi*.

MINAMOTO NO MUNEYUKI ASON

Yama zato wa
Fuyu zo sabishisa
Masari keru
Hito-me mo kusa mo
Karenu to omoeba.

源宗于朝臣

山里は冬ぞさびしさまさりける
人目も草もかれぬと思へば

THE MINISTER MUNEYUKI
MINAMOTO

THE mountain village solitude
  In winter time I dread;
It seems as if, when friends are gone,
  And trees their leaves have shed,
  All men and plants are dead.

The poet was a grandson of the Emperor Kwōkō, and died A.D. 940. The Minamoto family, who sprang from the Emperor Seiwa, who reigned 856–877, was at one time very powerful, and produced many famous men, including Yoritomo, the great founder of the Shōgunate. The Taira family and the Minamotos were the Yorks and Lancasters of mediaeval Japan; but, after thirty years of warfare, Yoritomo finally defeated his rivals in a great battle fought at Dan-no-ura, in the Straits of Shimonoseki, in 1185; the entire Taira family was exterminated, including women and children, and the infant Emperor Antoku. The Minamoto clan themselves became extinct in 1219, when Sanetomo was murdered at Kamakura, as related in the note to verse No. 93.

ŌSHI-KŌCHI NO MITSUNE

Kokoro-ate ni
Orabaya oramu
Hatsu shimo no
Oki madowaseru
Shira giku no hana.

凡河内躬恒

心あてに折らばや折らむはつ霜の
置きまどはせる白菊の花

MITSUNE ŌSHI-KŌCHI

IT was a white chrysanthemum
   I came to take away;
But, which are colored, which are white,
   I'm half afraid to say,
   So thick the frost to-day!

Mitsune lived some time in the beginning of the tenth century, and was one of the compilers of *Odes Ancient and Modern* (the *Kokinshiu*). The illustration shows him with a boy in attendance, trying to make up his mind which flower he will pick.

MIBU NO TADAMINE

Ariake no
Tsurenaku mieshi
Wakare yori
Akatsuki bakari
Uki-mono wa nashi.

壬生忠岑

有明のつれなく見えし別れより

暁ばかり憂きものはなし

TADAMINE MIBU

I HATE the cold unfriendly moon,
  That shines at early morn;
And nothing seems so sad and grey,
  When I am left forlorn,
  As day's returning dawn.

The writer lived to the age of ninety-nine, and died in the
year 965. He was, like the composer of the previous verse, one
of the compilers of the *Kokinshiu,* and was also the father of
the author of verse No. 41.

The picture seems to show the poet all alone looking out at
the early dawn, but the moon is not visible.

SAKA-NO-UYE NO KORENORI

Asaborake
Ariake no tsuki to
Miru made ni
Yoshino no sato ni
Fureru shira yuki.

さかのうえのこれのり
坂上是則

あさ　　　　ありあけ　つき
朝ぼらけ有明の月とみるまでに
よしの　　さと　　　　　　しらゆき
吉野の里にふれる白雪

KORENORI SAKA-NO-UYE

SURELY the morning moon, I thought,
  Has bathed the hill in light;
But, no; I see it is the snow
  That, falling in the night,
  Has made Yoshino white.

Little is known about this poet, but he is said to have lived some time in the tenth century. Yoshino is a mountain village in the Province of Yamato, famous for its cherry blossoms; at one time it contained the Imperial Summer Palace. In the illustration we see the poet looking across at the village on the hills all covered with snow.

HARUMICHI NO TSURAKI

Yama gawa ni
Kaze no kaketaru
Shigarami wa
Nagare mo aenu
Momiji nari keri.

はるみちのつらき
春道列樹

やまがは　かぜ
山川に風のかけたるしがらみは

なが　　　　　　　　もみぢ
流れもあへぬ紅葉なりけり

TSURAKI HARUMICHI

THE stormy winds of yesterday
  The maple branches shook;
And see! a mass of crimson leaves
  Has lodged within that nook,
  And choked the mountain brook.

The writer of this verse died in the year 864.

KI NO TOMONORI

Hisakata no
Hikari nodokeki
Haru no hi ni
Shizu kokoro naku
Hana no chiruramu.

<ruby>紀<rt>き</rt>友<rt>のとも</rt>則<rt>のり</rt></ruby>
紀友則

久方の光のどけき春の日に

しづ心なく花の散るらむ

TOMONORI KI

THE spring has come, and once again
   The sun shines in the sky;
So gently smile the heavens, that
   It almost makes me cry,
   When blossoms droop and die.

Tomonori Ki was the grandson of Uchisukune Take, a famous warrior, and nephew of Tsurayuki, who composed verse No. 35; he was one of the compilers of the *Kokinshiu,* and died at the beginning of the tenth century. He refers in this verse to the fall of the cherry blossoms.

Hisakata is a 'pillow-word' for heaven, without any definite meaning in the present day; it is generally used in poetry in conjunction with such words as sun, moon, sky, or, as in this case, 'the light' (of heaven).

The picture shows the poet with his attendant, watching the petals falling from the cherry tree.

FUJIWARA NO OKIKAZE

Tare wo ka mo
Shiru hito nisemu
Takasago no
Matsu mo mukashi no
Tomo nara-naku ni.

ふじわらのおきかぜ
藤原興風

し　　ひと　　　　たかさご
たれをかも知る人にせむ高砂の

まつ　むかし　とも
松も昔の友ならなくに

OKIKAZE FUJIWARA

GONE are my old familiar friends,
  The men I used to know;
Yet still on Takasago beach
  The same old pine trees grow,
  That I knew long ago.

Okikaze, the son of Michinari, was an official in the Province of Sagami in the year 911; the date of his death is unknown, but he is mentioned as being alive as late as the year 914. Takasago, which is mentioned again in verse No. 73, is a seaside place in the Province of Harima, famous for its pine trees; the pine tree is one of the recognized emblems of long life in Japan, because it is believed that after a thousand years its sap turns to amber.

KI NO TSURAYUKI

Hito wa iza
Kokoro mo shirazu
Furu sato wa
Hana zo mukashi no
Ka ni nioi keru.

きのゆらゆき
紀貫之

ひと　　　　こころ　し
人はいさ心も知らずふるさとは
はな　むかし　か
花ぞ昔の香ににほひける

TSURAYUKI KI

THE village of my youth is gone,
  New faces meet my gaze;
But still the blossoms at thy gate,
  Whose perfume scents the ways,
  Recall my childhood's days.

The writer of this verse, who lived A.D. 884–946, was a nobleman at Court, one of the greatest of the classical poets, and the first writer of Japanese prose. He was the chief compiler of the *Kokinshiu*, in which work he was assisted by the authors of verses Nos. 29, 30, and 33. This work consists of twenty volumes, containing some eleven hundred verses, and was completed in the year 922. It is related that Tsurayuki once visited a friend after a long absence; and on being asked jestingly by the latter, how he could remember the way after such a long interval of time, the poet broke off a spray of blossoms from a plum tree growing at the entrance, and presented it to his friend with this impromptu verse.

KIYOHARA NO FUKAYABU

Natsu no yo wa
Mada yoi nagara
Akenuru wo
Kumo no izuko ni
Tsuki yadoruramu.

きよはらのふかやぶ
清原深養父

夏の夜はまだ宵ながら明けぬるを
雲のいづこに月宿るらむ

FUKAYABU KIYOHARA

TOO short the lovely summer night,
  Too soon 'tis passed away;
I watched to see behind which cloud
  The moon would chance to stay,
  And here's the dawn of day!

Nothing is known of this writer, except that he was the
father of the author of verse No. 42.

FUNYA NO ASAYASU

Shira tsuyu ni
Kaze no fukishiku
Aki no no wa
Tsuranuki-tomenu
Tama zo chiri keru.

ふんやのあさやす
文屋朝康

しらつゆに風の吹きしく秋の野は

つらぬきとめぬ玉ぞ散りける

ASAYASU FUNYA

THIS lovely morn the dewdrops flash
  Like diamonds on the grass—
A blaze of sparkling jewels! But
  The autumn wind, alas!
  Scatters them as I pass.

Asayasu, the son of the author of verse No. 22, lived about the end of the ninth century. He is said to have composed this verse at the request of the Emperor Daigo in the year 900. To liken the dewdrops to jewels or beads (*tama*) is typical of Japanese verse. The picture shows the grass, and the dewdrops scattered on the ground in front of the poet.

UKON

Wasuraruru
Mi woba omowazu
Chikaite-shi
Hito no inochi no
Oshiku mo aru kana.

右近

わすらるる身をば思はず誓ひてし
人のいのちの惜しくもあるかな

UKON

MY broken heart I don't lament,
  To destiny I bow;
But thou hast broken solemn oaths,—
  I pray the Gods may now
  Absolve thee from thy vow.

The Lady Ukon is supposed to have been deserted by her husband, and in this poem she regrets, not so much her own sorrow, as the fact that he has broken his sworn oath, and is therefore in danger of divine vengeance. The illustration shows her all alone at the gate, with the house in the background, evidently waiting for the husband who has forsaken her.

SANGI HITOSHI

Asajū no
Ono no shinohara
Shinoburedo
Amarite nado ka
Hito no koishiki.

参議等

浅茅生の小野の篠原しのぶれど

あまりてなどか人の恋しき

THE PRIVY COUNCILLOR HITOSHI

'TIS easier to hide the reeds
Upon the moor that grow,
Than try to hide the ardent love
That sets my cheeks aglow
For somebody I know.

Little is known of Hitoshi Minamoto, except that he lived some time in the tenth century.

Note the word *shinohara*, meaning 'a bamboo moor', contrasted with *shinoburedo* in the next line, which means 'though I might manage to conceal'.

The picture shows Hitoshi on the wild moor, with the reeds growing all around him.

TAIRA NO KANEMORI

Shinoburedo
Iro ni ide ni keri
Waga koi wa
Mono ya omou to
Hito no tou made.

たいらのかねもり
平兼盛

忍ぶれど色にいでにけりわが恋は
ものや思ふと人の問ふまで

KANEMORI TAIRA

ALAS! the blush upon my cheek,
  Conceal it as I may,
Proclaims to all that I'm in love,
  Till people smile and say—
  'Where are thy thoughts to-day?'

This verse is said to have been composed in the year 960, at the request of the Emperor Murakami. Kanemori was the great-grandson of the Emperor Kwōtoku who is the writer of verse No. 15.

MIBU NO TADAMI

Koi su tefu
Waga na wa madaki
Tachi ni keri
Hito shirezu koso
Omoi-someshi ka.

壬生忠見

恋すてふわが名はまだき立ちにけり

人しれずこそ思ひそめしか

TADAMI MIBU

OUR courtship, that we tried to hide,
  Misleading is to none;
And yet how could the neighbors guess,
  That I had yet begun
  To fancy any one?

The poet was the son of the writer of verse No. 30, and he is said to have composed the poem on the same occasion as is mentioned for No. 40.

The word *omoi* in the last line is a 'pivot–word', used firstly in connection with the fourth line, meaning 'I thought' (nobody knew), and also in conjunction with *someshi*, where it means 'I began to be in love'.

KIYOHARA NO MOTOSUKE

Chigiriki na
Katami-ni sode wo
Shibori-tsutsu
Sue no Matsu-yama
Nami kosaji to wa.

きよはらのもとすけ
清原元輔

ちぎ　　　　　　　　　　　そで
契りきなかたみに袖をしぼりつつ

すゑ　まつやま　　　こ
末の松山なみ越さじとは

MOTOSUKE KIYOHARA

OUR sleeves, all wet with tears, attest
That you and I agree
That to each other we'll be true,
Till Pine-tree Hill shall be
Sunk far beneath the sea.

Motosuke lived towards the close of the tenth century, and was the son of the writer of verse No. 36. The idea of one's sleeves being wet with tears is a common one in Japanese poetry. Matsu-yama, or Pine-tree Hill, is in Northern Japan, on the boundaries between the Provinces of Rikuchū and Nambu. In the illustration the hill with the pine tree on the top appears to be just sinking beneath the waves.

CHŪ-NAGON ATSUTADA

Ai-mite no
Nochi no kokoro ni
Kurabureba
Mukashi wa mono wo
Omowazari keri.

権中納言敦忠

あひみてののちの心にくらぶれば

昔はものを思はざりけり

THE IMPERIAL ADVISER ATSUTADA

HOW desolate my former life,
  Those dismal years, ere yet
I chanced to see thee face to face;
  'Twere better to forget
  Those days before we met.

Atsutada was a member of the great Fujiwara family, and is said to have died in the year 943.

It is interesting to note in these illustrations, as in nearly all old Japanese pictures, that the artist either takes off the roof of the house or removes part of the wall when he wishes you to see what is going on indoors.

CHŪ-NAGON ASATADA

Au koto no
Taete shi nakuba
　Naka naka ni
Hito wo mo mi wo mo
Uramizaramashi.

<ruby>中納言朝忠<rt>ちゅうなごんあさただ</rt></ruby>

逢ふことの絶えてしなくばなかなかに
人をも身をも恨みざらまし

THE IMPERIAL ADVISER ASATADA

TO fall in love with womankind
  Is my unlucky fate;
If only it were otherwise,
  I might appreciate
  Some men, whom now I hate.

The writer of this verse was the son of Sadakata, a Minister-of-the-Right, and is said to have died in the year 961. The verse was composed at the instance of the Emperor Daigo, and is apparently written in praise of a life of single blessedness. The translation does not give the full force of the last two lines, which mean literally, 'I should not dislike both other people and myself too.' The illustration shows Asatada walking on the verandah outside his house, perhaps composing this verse.

KENTOKU KŌ

Aware to mo
Iu beki hito wa
Omohoede
Mi no itazura ni
Narinu beki kana.

けんとくこう
謙徳公

あはれともいふべき人は思ほえで
身のいたづらになりぬべきかな

PRINCE KENTOKU

I DARE not hope my lady-love
　　Will smile on me again;
She knows no pity, and my life
　　I care not to retain,
　　Since all my prayers are vain.

The real name of the witer of this verse was Koretada Fujiwara; he died in the year 972, and Prince Kentoku is his posthumous name.

Aware to mo means, in conjunction with the next line, 'that she would give me words of pity'; but *aware tomo* can also mean 'to meet as a friend'.

In spite of the Prince's fears, the illustration seems to suggest that his lady-love changed her mind, and came to visit him once more.

SONE NO YOSHITADA

Yura no to wo
Wataru funabito
Kaji wo tae
Yukue mo shiranu
Koi no michi kana.

そねのよしただ
曾禰好忠

ゆら と わたる ふなびと た
由良の門を渡る舟人かぢを絶え
ゆくへ し こひ
行方も知らぬ恋のみちかな

YOSHITADA SONE

THE fishing-boats are tossed about,
  When stormy winds blow strong;
With rudder lost, how can they reach
  The port for which they long?
  So runs the old love-song.

Nothing is known of the writer of this verse, but he is said
to have lived in the tenth century. The meaning, not very clear-
ly expressed in the translation, is that the course of true love is
as uncertain as the course of the rudderless fishing-boats. In the
illustration we see the fishing-boat tossing about on a rough sea
and the rudder duly floating away astern.

YEGYŌ HŌSHI

Yaemugura
Shigereru yado no
Sabishiki ni
Hito koso miene
Aki wa ki ni keri.

恵慶法師

八重むぐらしげれる宿のさびしきに
人こそ見えね秋は来にけり

THE PRIEST YEGYŌ

MY little temple stands alone,
　No other hut is near;
No one will pass to stop and praise
　Its vine-grown roof, I fear,
　Now that the autumn's here.

The Priest Yegyō lived about the end of the tenth century, but nothing is known about him. In the picture he is shown outside his humble little temple with its patched roof and the vine growing up the wall.

MINAMOTO NO SHIGEYUKI

Kaze wo itami
Iwa utsu nami no
Onore nomi
Kudakete mono wo
Omou koro kana.

<ruby>源<rt>みなもと</rt></ruby>重え

みなもとのしげゆき
源重え

風をいたみ岩うつ波のおのれのみ

くだけてものを思ふころかな

SHIGEYUKI MINAMOTO

THE waves that dash against the rocks
　　Are broken by the wind
And turned to spray; my loving heart
　　Is broken too, I find,
　　Since thou art so unkind.

The writer of this verse is said to have died in the year 963; for a note about the great Minamoto family, see verse No. 28. In the picture we see Shigeyuki, with an attendant carrying his sword, walking on the shore, while the waves break into spray at his feet.

ŌNAKATOMI NO YOSHINOBU ASON

Mikaki mori
Eji no taku hi no
Yoru wa moe
Hiru wa kie-tsutsu
Mono wo koso omoe.

大中臣能宣朝臣

みかきもり衛士のたく火の夜はもえ
昼は消えつつものをこそ思へ

THE MINISTER YOSHINOBU, OF PRIESTLY RANK

MY constancy to her I love
I never will forsake;
As surely as the Palace Guards
Each night their watch-fire make
And guard it till daybreak.

The author was the son of the Minister Yorimoto, and he lived during the latter part of the tenth century. The illustration shows the watchman outside the Palace tending his fire.

FUJIWARA NO YOSHITAKA

Kimi ga tame
Oshikarazarishi
Inochi sae
Nagaku mogana to
Omoi keru kana.

藤原義孝

君がため惜しからざりし命さへ

長くもがなと思ひけるかな

YOSHITAKA FUJIWARA

DEATH had no terrors, Life no joys,
  Before I met with thee;
But now I fear, however long
  My life may chance to be,
  'Twill be too short for me!

Yoshitaka died in the year 974. See verse No. 18 for a note of the Fujiwara family.

FUJIWARA NO SANEKATA ASON

Kaku to dani
Eyawa Ibuki no
Sashi-mogusa
Sashimo shiraji na
Moyuru omoi wo.

藤原実方朝臣

かくとだにえやはいぶきのさしも草
さしも知らじな燃ゆる思ひを

THE MINISTER SANEKATA FUJIWARA

THOUGH love, like blisters made from leaves
  Grown on Mount Ibuki,
Torments me more than I can say,
  My lady shall not see,
  How she is paining me.

The writer lived some time at the close of the tenth century. The artemisia plant (or mugwort) is used in Japan for cauterizing; a conical wad of the leaves or blossoms is placed on the spot, lit at the top, and allowed to burn down to the skin; this produces a blister, and is extremely painful. Ibuki is a hill, between the Provinces of Omi and Mino, famous for its artemisia, but *ibuki* can also stand for *iu beki,* which, in conjunction with *e ya wa,* would mean, 'Ah! how could I tell her!' But *eyawa* as one word means 'indescribable!' Notice also *sashimo* in the third and fourth lines; *sashi-mogusa* means 'the artemisia plant', but *sashi mo* means 'even though it is smarting'; *sashimo,* in one word, can also mean 'in such a way'. This verse is a very good example of the way the Japanese love to play upon words. The picture seems to show Mount Ibuki with the mugwort growing on it.

FUJIWARA NO MICHINOBU ASON

Akenureba
Kururu mono to wa
Shiri nagara
Nao urameshiki
Asaborake kana.

ふじわらのみちのぶあそん
藤原道信朝臣

明けぬれば暮るるものとは知りながら

なほ恨めしき朝ぼらけかな

THE MINISTER MICHINOBU FUJIWARA

ALTHOUGH I know the gentle night
   Will surely follow morn,
Yet, when I'm wakened by the sun,
   Turn over, stretch and yawn—
   How I detest the dawn!

Michinobu lived in the tenth century. He is shown in the illustration with his wife on the verandah, watching the day break.

UDAISHŌ MICHITSUNA NO HAHA

Nageki-tsutsu
Hitori nuru yo no
Akuru ma wa
Ikani hisashiki
Mono to kawa shiru.

<ruby>右大将道綱母<rt>うだいしょうみちつなのはは</rt></ruby>

なげきつつひとりぬる夜の明くるまは
いかに久しきものとかは知る

THE MOTHER OF MICHITSUNA, COMMANDER OF THE RIGHT IMPERIAL GUARDS

ALL through the long and dreary night
  I lie awake and moan;
How desolate my chamber feels,
  How weary I have grown
  Of being left alone!

This lady was the daughter of Motoyasu Fujiwara, and the wife of the Regent Kaneie; she was famous for her beauty, and lived in the reign of the Emperor Murakami (947–967). It is related, that her husband returned home late one night, and, having to wait a moment or two before she let him in, he angrily reproached her, and she replied with this verse (see illustration).

Yo no akuru ma means 'until the dawn', but *akuru ma* also suggests that the room is empty when he is away.

GIDŌ-SANSHI NO HAHA

Wasureji no
Yukusue made wa
Katakereba
Kyō wo kagiri no
Inochi tomo gana.

儀同三司母

わすれじの行末まではかたければ

今日をかぎりの命ともがな

THE MOTHER OF THE MINISTER
OF STATE

HOW difficult it is for men
Not to forget the past!
I fear my husband's love for me
Is disappearing fast;
This day must be my last.

The real name of this lady was Taka, and her son's name
was Korechika Fujiwara. She lived about A.D. 1004, and it is
supposed that this verse was written in a fit of jealousy against
her husband; she is shown in the picture all alone at home
bewailing her lot.

DAI-NAGON KINTŌ

Taki no oto wa
Taete hisashiku
Narinuredo
Na koso nagarete
Nao kikoe kere.

だいなごんきんとう
大納言公任

たき おと　　　　　　　　ひさ
瀧の音はたえて久しくなりぬれど
な　　　なが　　　　　きこ
名こそ流れてなほ聞えけれ

THE FIRST ADVISER OF STATE KINTŌ

THIS waterfall's melodious voice
  Was famed both far and near;
Although it long has ceased to flow,
  Yet still with memory's ear
  Its gentle splash I hear.

This poet was the father of the writer of verse No. 64, and was a member of the Fujiwara family at the zenith of their power; he was a great statesman and scholar, and died in the year 1041. The verse was written in praise of a waterfall that had been made by the orders of the Emperor Saga early in the ninth century, but which had by this time ceased to exist; and the illustration well shows the watercourse now run dry.

IZUMI SHIKIBU

Arazaramu
Kono yo no hoka no
Omoide ni
Ima hito tabi no
Au koto mo gana.

和泉式部

あらざらむこの世のほかの思ひ出に
いまひとたびの逢ふこともがな

IZUMI SHIKIBU

MY life is drawing to a close,
  I cannot longer stay,
A pleasant memory of thee
  I fain would take away;
  So visit me, I pray.

This lady was the daughter of Masamine Ōye, and the wife of Michisada Tachibana, Governor of the Province of Izumi, hence her name; and also was the mother of the author of verse No. 60. She lived about the latter end of the tenth century, and was one of the lady poets who gave distinction to that period. The verse was addressed to her husband or lover just before her death, and in the illustration we see her on her deathbed, with two servants in the foreground.

MURASAKI SHIKIBU

Meguri-aite
Mishi ya sore tomo
Wakanu ma ni
Kumo gakure nishi
Yowa no tsuki kana.

紫式部

めぐりあひて見しやそれとも分かぬまに
雲がくれにし夜半の月影

MURASAKI SHIKIBU

I WANDERED forth this moonlight night,
  And some one hurried by;
But who it was I could not see,—
  Clouds driving o'er the sky
  Obscured the moon on high.

This lady lost her mother when very young, and her father,
the minister Toyonari Fujiwara, married again. Her skill at
composing verses caused her stepmother to become jealous,
and the latter treated her with great cruelty. She married
Nobutaka, a nobleman, and the following verse was written by
her daughter. She is famous in Japanese literature as the
authoress of *Genji Monogatari*, a historical work in fifty-four
sections, which she wrote in the monastery of Ishiyama, near
Kyōto. She was one night taking a moonlight stroll on her
verandah and caught sight of her lover; but, though she barely
recognized him, the *Kokinshiu*, from which the verse is taken,
adds that you are to understand that her reputation was over-
shadowed from that moment, like the moon behind the clouds.
She died in the year 992.

  Sore tomo can mean either 'though I glanced at him', or else
(*wakanu*, I did not recognize) 'that friend'.

DAINI NO SAMMI

Arima yama
Ina no sasahara
Kaze fukeba
Ide soyo hito wo
Wasure yawa suru.

大弐三位

有馬山猪名のささ原風吹けば

いでそよ人を忘れやはする

DAINI NO SAMMI

AS fickle as the mountain gusts
   That on the moor I've met,
'Twere best to think no more of thee,
   And let thee go. But yet
   I never can forget.

The name given above is only a title, and the real name of this lady is unknown; she was the daughter of the writer of the previous verse, and the wife of Daini Nariakira. The picture shows her on the moor composing the verse. Note the echoing sound in the last line, '*Wasure yawa suru.*'

AKAZOME EMON

Yasurawade
Nenamashi mono wo
Sayofukete
Katabuku made no
Tsuki wo mishi kana.

赤染衛門

やすらはで寝なましものを小夜更けて
かたぶくまでの月を見しかな

AKAZOME EMON

WAITING and hoping for thy step,
  Sleepless in bed I lie,
All through the night, until the moon,
  Leaving her post on high,
  Slips sideways down the sky.

This writer is again a lady; she is said to have addressed the verse to Michinaga Fujiwara, who held the office of Regent under the Emperor Ichijō (A.D. 987–1011) and his two successors. Regent here must be understood not exactly as a temporary or vice Emperor, but rather as the Emperor's confidential adviser, and the official through whom all communications were made. Notice the moon in the illustration just disappearing behind the hill.

KO-SHIKIBU NO NAISHI

Ohoye yama
Ikuno no michi no
　Tohokereba
Mada fumi mo mizu
Ama-no-Hashidate.

<ruby>小式部内侍<rt>こしきぶのないし</rt></ruby>

大江山いく野の道の遠ければ

まだふみも見ず天の橋立

LADY-IN-WAITING KO-SHIKIBU

SO long and dreary is the road,
That I have never been
To Ama-no-Hashidate;
Pray, how could I have seen
The verses that you mean?

Koshikibu was the daughter of the writer of verse No. 56, and early became known as a poetess. The story goes, that she was suspected of getting help from her mother in composing poetry; and on one occasion, during the absence of the latter at Ama-no-Hashidate, she was selected to take part in a poetical contest at Court. A day or two before the event a nobleman laughingly asked her, if she was not expecting a letter from her mother, hinting that she would otherwise be unable to produce a poem good enough for the contest, and she, touching his sleeve, improvised the above verse. The original brings in not only Ama-no-Hashidate, a picturesque bay in the Province of Tango, but also two other proper names, Mount Ohoye and Ikuno, which are on the road there from Kyōto; but this the translation fails to do.

The last couplet can mean 'I have not walked to or seen Ama-no-Hashidate' , and also, 'I have not seen any letter from Ama-no-Hashidate.'

ISE NO DAIFU

Inishie no
Nara no Miyako no
Yaezakura
Kyō kokonoe ni
Nioi nuru kana.

<ruby>伊勢大輔<rt>いせのだいふ</rt></ruby>

いにしへの<ruby>奈良<rt>なら</rt></ruby>の<ruby>都<rt>みやこ</rt></ruby>の<ruby>八重桜<rt>やへざくら</rt></ruby>

けふ<ruby>九重<rt>こののへ</rt></ruby>にほひぬるかな

THE LADY ISE

THE double cherry trees, which grew
　At Nara in past days,
Now beautify this Palace, and
　Their blossoms all ablaze
　Perfume the royal ways.

　The Lady Ise was another of the famous literary women, that distinguished the Imperial Court at the end of the tenth century; she was associated with the Province of Ise, from which she gets her name. Nara was the capital city from A.D. 709 to 784, after which the Court moved to Kyōto. It is related, that during the reign of the Emperor Ichijō (A.D. 987–1011) a nobleman presented him with a spray of the eight-petalled cherry trees that grew at Nara; the Emperor was so delighted, that he had the trees, or perhaps cuttings from them, brought to Kyōto, and this verse commemorates the event.

　Kokonoe (Palace) really means 'ninefold', and refers to the nine enclosures of the Imperial Residence; it is here contrasted with *yaezakura*, the eightfold or double cherry blossom.

SEI SHŌ-NAGON

Yo wo komete
Tori no sorane wa
Hakaru tomo
Yo ni Ausaka no
Seki wa yurusaji.

清少納言

夜をこめて鳥の空音ははかるとも

よに逢坂の関はゆるさじ

THE LADY SEI

TOO long to-night you've lingered here,
  And, though you imitate
The crowing of a cock, 'twill not
  Unlock the tollbar gate;
  Till daylight must you wait.

The Lady Sei, Shō-nagon being merely a title, was the daughter of the writer of verse No. 42, and the authoress of *Makura-no-Sōshi*, or 'A story book to keep under one's pillow'; she was, with the writer of verse No. 57, one of the greatest of Japanese authors. She was a lady-in-waiting at Court, and retired to a convent in the year 1000. This verse has reference to the Chinese story of Prince Tan Chu, who was shut up with his retainers in the town of Kankokkan; the city gates were closed from sunset to cockcrow, but during the night one of the Prince's followers so successfully imitated the crowing of a cock, that the guards, thinking it was daybreak, opened the gates, and the fugitives escaped under cover of the darkness. It is related, that the Emperor once noticed Lady Sei admiring the freshly fallen snow, and asked 'How is the snow of Kōrohō?' She at once raised the window curtain, showing that she recognized the allusion to the verse 'The snow of Kōrohō is seen by raising the curtain'.

SANKYŌ NO DAIBU MICHIMASA

Ima wa tada
Omoi-taenamu
Tobakari wo
Hitozute narade
Iu yoshi mo gana.

さきょうのだいぶみちまさ
左京大夫道雅

いま　　　　おも　た
今はただ思ひ絶えなむとばかりを
ひと
人づてならでいふよしもがな

THE SHINTO OFFICIAL MICHIMASA, OF THE LEFT SIDE OF THE CAPITAL

IF we could meet in privacy,
Where no one else could see,
Softly I'd whisper in thy ear
This little word from me—
'I'm dying, Love, for thee.'

Michimasa was a member of the Fujiwara family, who lived about the year 1030. He fell in love with the Princess Masako, a priestess of Ise; but when the Emperor heard of this, he put the Princess into confinement, where she was strictly guarded by female warders, and this verse was Michimasa's request to her to try to arrange a private meeting with him. The words *omoi-taenamu*, which is the message he sends to her, mean, 'I shall die of love'; but they can also mean 'I shall think no more about you'; so perhaps he intended the verse to be read in different ways, according to whether it reached the Princess, or fell into the hands of her guards. In the picture Michimasa is shown outside the fortress, where the Princess is confined.

GON CHŪ-NAGON SADAYORI

Asaborake
Uji no kawagiri
Tae-dae ni
Araware wataru
Seze no ajiro-gi.

権中納言定頼

朝ぼらけ宇治の川霧たえだえに

あらはれ渡る瀬々の網代木

THE ASSISTANT IMPERIAL ADVISER SADAYORI

So thickly lies the morning mist,
  That I can scarcely see
The fish-nets on the river bank,
  The River of Uji,
  Past daybreak though it be.

The writer was the son of the author of verse No. 55; he died in the year 1004. The River Uji is in the Province of Omi, and drains into Lake Biwa. Seze is a village on the lake-side, and a suburb of the larger town of Otsu. The poet, looking across the river, can hardly make out the fish-nets on the shore at Seze, because of the rising morning mist.

SAGAMI

Urami wabi
Hosanu sode dani
Aru mono wo
Koi ni kuchinamu
Na koso oshikere.

相模

恨みわびほさぬ袖だにあるものを
恋にくちなむ名こそ惜しけれ

SAGAMI

BE not displeased, but pardon me,
  If still my tears o'erflow;
My lover's gone, and my good name,
  Which once I valued so,
  I fear must also go.

This lady was the wife of Kinsuke Ōye, the Governor of the Province of Sagami, from which she got her name. The verse is said to have been composed at an Imperial poetical contest in the year 1051. The incidents mentioned in these verses are not all supposed to have really taken place; many of the poems, including this one, were simply written on a given subject for one of the poetical contests, which were so common at the period.

DAISŌJŌ GYŌSON

Morotomo ni
Aware to omoe
Yama zakura
Hana yori hoka ni
Shiru hito mo nashi.

大僧正行尊

もろともにあはれと思へ山桜
花よりほかに知る人もなし

THE ARCHBISHOP GYŌSON

IN lonely solitude I dwell,
  No human face I see;
And so we two must sympathize,
  Oh mountain cherry tree;
  I have no friend but thee.

The Archbishop is said to have ended his life in the year 1135, by the method described in the note to verse No. 12. The scene of this poem was the scared mountain Ōmine, in the Province of Yamato, famous for its cherry blossoms, and the illustration shows the Priest with his two attendants addressing the cherry tree.

SWŌ NO NAISHI

Haru no yo no
Yume bakari naru
Ta-makura ni
Kainaku tatamu
Na koso oshi kere.

<ruby>周防内侍<rt>すおうのないし</rt></ruby>

春の夜の夢ばかりなる手枕に
かひなく立たむ名こそ惜しけれ

THE LADY-IN-WAITING SWŌ

IF I had made thy proffered arm
  A pillow for my head
For but the moment's time, in which
  A summer's dream had fled,
  What would the world have said?

The authoress was the daughter of Tsugunaka Taira, the Governor of the Province of Suwo, and a lady-in-waiting at the Court of the Emperor Goreizei, who reigned A.D. 1046–1068. She was present one day at a long and tedious court function, and, feeling very tired and sleepy, she called to a servant for a pillow; a nobleman on the other side of the screen, the First Adviser of State Tadaie, gallantly offered her his arm, with a request that she would rest her head there, and she replied with this verse. She intended him to understand that, though she was willing to accept him as her husband for life, she feared that his attachment would last no longer than a fleeting summernight's dream.

SANJŌ IN

Kokoro ni mo
Arade uki yo ni
Nagaraeba
Koishikarubeki
Yowa no tsuki kana.

三条院

心にもあらでうき世にながらへば
恋しかるべき夜半の月かな

THE RETIRED EMPEROR SANJŌ

IF in this troubled world of ours
I still must linger on,
My only friend shall be the moon,
Which on my sadness shone,
When other friends were gone.

The Emperor Sanjō, who reigned A.D. 1012–1015, was the son of the Emperor Reisei; he fell into ill health, his palace was burnt down twice, and he was forced to abdicate by Michinaga Fujiwara (see verse No. 59).

NŌIN HŌSHI

Arashi fuku
Mimuro no yama no
Momiji-ba wa
Tatsuta no kawa no
Nishiki nari keri.

能因法師

嵐吹く三室の山のもみぢ葉は

竜田の川の錦なりけり

THE PRIEST NŌIN

THE storms, which round Mount Mimuro
    Are wont to howl and scream,
Have thickly scattered maple leaves
    Upon Tatsuta's stream;
    Like red brocade they seem.

The poet's lay name was Nagayasu Tachibana; he was the son of Motoyasu Tachibana, the Governor of the Province of Hizen. Mount Mimuro and the Tatsuta River are both in the Province of Yamato, not far from Nara. The picture is not very clear, but the river is plainly depicted, and maple leaves are scattered all around.

RYŌZEN HŌSHI

Sabishisa ni
Yado wo tachi-idete
Nagamureba
Izuku mo onaji
Aki no yūgure.

りょうぜんほうし
良暹法師

やど　た　い
さびしさに宿を立ち出でてながむれば

おな　あき　ゆうぐれ
いづくも同じ秋の夕暮

THE PRIEST RYŌZEN

THE prospect from my cottage shows
  No other hut in sight;
The solitude depresses me,
  Like deepening twilight
  On a chill autumn night.

Nothing is known of this author, but he appears to have lived during the eleventh century. The Priest appears in the illustration, looking out over the bare landscape, with his tiny hut in the background.

DAI-NAGON TSUNENOBU

Yūsareba
Kado-ta no inaba
Otozurete
Ashi no maroya ni
Aki kaze zo fuku.

大納言経信

夕されば門田の稲葉おとづれて

蘆のまろ屋に秋風ぞ吹く

THE FIRST ADVISER OF STATE
TSUNENOBU

THIS autumn night the wind blows shrill,
  And would that I could catch
Its message, as it whistles through
  The rushes in the thatch
  And leaves of my rice-patch.

Tsunenobu, a member of the Minamoto family, was famous as a man of letters in the eleventh century, and died in the year 1096.

YŪSHI NAISHINNŌ-KE NO KI

Oto ni kiku
Takashi no hama no
Adanami wa
Kakeji ya sode no
Nure mo koso sure.

祐子内親王家紀伊

音にきく高師の浜のあだ波は

かけじや袖の濡れもこそすれ

THE LADY KI, OF THE HOUSE OF PRINCESS YŪSHI

THE sound of ripples on the shore
    Ne'er fails at Takashi;
My sleeves all worn and wet with tears
    Should surely prove to thee,
    I, too, will constant be.

The Lady Ki lived at the Court of the Emperor Horikawa, who reigned A.D. 1087–1107. Takashi is a seaside place in the Province of Izumi, not far from Ōsaka, and on the shore we see the Lady Ki, perhaps composing this verse to her lover.

GON CHŪ-NAGON MASAFUSA

Takasago no
Onoe no sakura
Saki ni keri
Toyama no kasumi
Tatazu mo aranamu.

権中納言匡房

高砂の尾上の桜咲きにけり

外山の霞立たずもあらなむ

THE ASSISTANT IMPERIAL ADVISER MASAFUSA

THE cherry trees are blossoming
  On Takasago's height;
Oh may no mountain mist arise,
  No clouds so soft and white,
  To hide them from our sight.

This poet was the son of Chikanari Ooi, and died in the year 1112. Takasago is on the sea-coast in the Province of Harima, and is also mentioned in verse No. 34.

Masafusa with his attendant appears in the illustration admiring the cherry trees on the mountains, over which, however, the clouds are already beginning to gather.

MINAMOTO NO TOSHIYORI ASON

Ukari keru
Hito wo Hatsuse no
Yama-oroshi yo
Hageshikare to wa
Inoranu mono wo.

<ruby>源俊頼朝臣<rt>みなもとのとしよりあそん</rt></ruby>
源俊頼朝臣

憂かりける人をはつせの山おろしよ

はげしかれとは祈らぬものを

THE MINISTER TOSHIYORI MINAMOTO

OH! Kwannon, Patron of this hill,
The maid, for whom I pine,
Is obstinate and wayward, like
The gusts around thy shrine.
What of those prayers of mine?

Toshiyori is supposed to have been the son of the writer of verse No. 71; he probably lived early in the twelfth century. Hatsuse is a mountain village near Nara, in the Province of Yamato; the temple there is dedicated to Kwannon, Goddess of Mercy, 'who looketh for ever down above the sound of prayer.'

FUJIWARA NO MOTOTOSHI

Chigiri okishi
Sasemo ga tsuyu wo
Inochi nite
Aware kotoshi no
Aki mo inumeri.

ふじわらのもととし
藤原基俊

ちぎり　　　　　　　　　つゆ　いのち
契りおきしさせもが露を命にて
　　　　　　　　ことし　あき
あはれ今年の秋もいぬめり

MOTOTOSHI FUJIWARA

IT is a promise unfulfilled,
  For which I humbly sue;
The dainty little mugwort plant
  Relies upon the dew,
  And I rely—on you.

The writer lived early in the twelfth century, when the Court was given over to intrigue. Tadamichi Fujiwara, the Regent, had promised him a post of honor for his son, but had, year after year, failed to fulfil it. The verse is a gentle reminder, and the last couplet, which does not appear in the translation, delicately hints that the autumn of the present year also is slipping away. In the illustration we see Mototoshi addressing his petition to the Regent.

HŌSHŌ-JI NYŪDŌ SAKI NO KWAMPAKU DAIJŌDAIJIN

Wata no hara
Kogi idete mireba
Hisakata no
Kumoi ni magau
Okitsu shira nami.

法性寺入道前関白太政大臣

わたの原漕ぎ出でてみれば久方の

雲居にまがふ沖つ白波

THE LATE REGENT AND PRIME MINISTER, THE LAY PRIEST OF THE HŌSHŌ TEMPLE

WHEN rowing on the open sea,
The waves, all capped with white,
Roll onward, like the fleecy clouds
With their resistless might;
Truly a wondrous sight!

The real name of this poet was Tadamichi Fujiwara, mentioned in connection with the previous verse, who retired from the world and entered the church. He was the father of the author of verse No. 95, and is supposed to have died in the year 1164, at the age of sixty-eight.

The 'pillow-word' *hisakata*, here used in connection with the clouds, is referred to in the note to verse No. 33.

SUTOKU IN

Se wo hayami
Iwa ni sekaruru
Taki-gawa no
Warete mo sue ni
Awamu to zo omō.

崇徳院

瀬をはやみ岩にせかるる滝川の
われても末にあはむとぞ思ふ

THE RETIRED EMPEROR SUTOKU

THE rock divides the stream in two,
  And both with might and main
Go tumbling down the waterfall;
  But well I know the twain
  Will soon unite again.

The town of Kamakura, where is the great bronze image of
Buddha Amida, was built by this Emperor, who reigned A.D.
1124–1141; he was then forced by his father, the ex-Emperor
Toba, to abdicate in favor of his brother, the Emperor Konoye;
afterwards he entered the church, and died in the year 1164, an
exile in the Province of Sanuki. This verse is intended to sug-
gest the parting of two lovers, who will eventually meet again.

MINAMOTO NO KANEMASA

Awaji shima
Kayou chidori no
Naku koe ni
Iku yo nezamenu
Suma no seki-mori.

源兼昌

淡路島かよふ千鳥のなく声に

幾夜寝ざめぬ須磨の関守

KANEMASA MINAMOTO

BETWEEN Awaji and the shore
 The birds scream in their flight;
Full oft they've made the Suma Guard
 Toss through a sleepless night,
 Until the morning light.

The writer was the son of Kanesuke, and died about the year 1112. *Chidori* are snipe or plovers, but here are apparently meant for seagulls. Awaji is a large island in the Inland Sea, near Kobe, and Suma is a point on the mainland in the Province of Settsu, immediately opposite.

SAKYŌ NO DAIBU AKISUKE

Aki kaze ni
Tanabiku kumo no
Taema yori
More-izuru tsuki no
Kage no sayakesa.

左京大夫顕輔

秋風にたなびく雲の絶えまより
もれ出づる月の影のさやけさ

THE SHINTO OFFICIAL AKISUKE, OF THE LEFT SIDE OF THE CAPITAL

SEE, how the wind of autumn drives
The clouds to left and right,
While in between the moon peeps out,
Dispersing with her light
The darkness of the night.

Akisuke died about the year 1155. *More-izuru* literally means, that the light of the moon 'leaks out'; the verse is a charming example of a Japanese picture-poem. Probably the first word of the verse was purposely made to coincide with the poet's first name in sound, although the two words are written with different characters in the original.

TAIKEN MON-IN NO HORIKAWA

Nagakaramu
Kokoro mo shirazu
Kuro kami no
Midarete kesa wa
Mono wo koso omoe.

待賢門院堀河

長からむ心も知らず黒髪の

みだれて今朝はものをこそ思へ

LADY HORIKAWA, IN ATTENDANCE ON THE DOWAGER EMPRESS TAIKEN

MY doubt about his constancy
Is difficult to bear;
Tangled this morning are my thoughts,
As is my long black hair.
I wonder—Does he care?

Lady Horikawa was the daughter of the First Adviser of State, Sane-kyo, who lived about the year 1142. In this verse she is anxiously pondering, how long her lover will continue to be true to her; and she discovers, that her ideas on the subject are as tangled and disordered as her hair is.

GO TOKUDAI-JI NO SADAIJIN

Hototogisu
Nakitsuru kata wo
Nagamureba
Tada ariake no
Tsuki zo nokoreru.

後徳大寺左大臣

ほととぎす鳴きつる方をながむれば

ただ有明の月ぞ残れる

THE MINISTER-OF-THE-LEFT OF THE TOKUDAI TEMPLE

THE cuckoo's echo dies away,
 And lo! the branch is bare;
I only see the morning moon,
 Whose light is fading there
 Before the daylight's glare.

The writer's name was Sanesada Fujiwara, and he entered the priesthood in the year 1198. The cuckoo, according to Japanese tradition, cries through the night until its eyes become bloodshot. It is supposed to come from the Spirit-land across the mountains of Hades, about the end of the fifth month, to warn the farmer that it is time to sow his rice. In the illustration we see the morning moon setting behind the hills, and the cuckoo flying away.

DŌIN HŌSHI

Omoi-wabi
Satemo inochi wa
Aru mono wo
Uki ni taenu wa
Namida nari keri.

どういんほうし
道因法師

おも　　　　　　　　いのち
思ひわびさても命はあるものを
う　　　　　　　　　　なみだ
憂きにたへぬは涙なりけり

THE PRIEST DŌIN

HOW sad and gloomy is the world,
  This world of sin and woe!
Ah! while I drift along Life's stream,
  Tossed helpless to and fro,
  My tears will ever flow.

The Priest Dōin was a member of the Fujiwara family. The date of this verse is not known, but it was probably written in the twelfth century. The illustration shows the priest alone in his hut, lamenting over the sorrows of humanity.

KWŌ-TAI-KŌGŪ NO DAIBU
SHUNZEI

Yo no naka yo
Michi koso nakere
Omoi iru
Yama no oku ni mo
Shika zo naku naru.

こうたいごうぐうのたいぶしゅんぜい
皇太后宮大夫俊成

よ　なか　みち　　　　　　　　おも　　い
世の中よ道こそなけれ思ひ入る

やま　おく　　　しか　　な
山の奥にも鹿ぞ鳴くなる

SHUNZEI, A SHINTO OFFICIAL IN ATTENDANCE ON THE EMPRESS DOWAGER

FROM pain and sorrow all around
There's no escape, I fear;
To mountain wilds should I retreat,
There also I should hear
The cry of hunted deer.

Shunzei was a celebrated poet and nobleman in the reign of the Emperor Gotoba. He, however, gave up his position at Court and entered the church in the year 1176. He was the father of the writers of verses Nos. 94 and 97, and died in the year 1204, at the age of ninety-one.

FUJIWARA NO KIYOSUKE ASON

Nagaraeba
Mata konogoro ya
Shinobaremu
Ushi to mishi yo zo
Ima wa koishiki.

藤原清輔朝臣

ながらへばまたこのごろやしのばれむ

憂しと見し世ぞいまは恋しき

THE MINISTER KIYOSUKE FUJIWARA

TIME was when I despised my youth,
　　As boyhood only can;
What would I give for boyhood now,
　　When finishing life's span
　　An old decrepid man!

Kiyosuke was the son of the writer of verse No. 79, and lived in the latter part of the twelfth century.

SHUN-YE HŌSHI

Yomosugara
Mono omou koro wa
Ake yarade
Neya no hima sae
Tsurena kari keri.

俊恵法師

夜もすがらもの思ふころは明けやらで
閨のひまさへつれなかりけり

THE PRIEST SHUN-YE

ALL through the never-ending night
  I lie awake and think;
In vain I look to try and see
  The daybreak's feeble blink
  Peep through the shutter's chink.

This priest was the son of the author of verse No. 74. He describes in this poem a sleepless night, when he looks in vain to catch the first glimpse of daybreak through the joints of the sliding screens, that form the walls of a Japanese house. But in the picture, as will be noticed, one of the sliding screens is removed, in order to show the priest within.

SAIGYŌ HŌSHI

Nageke tote
Tsuki ya wa mono wo
Omowasuru
Kakochi-gao naru
Waga namida kana.

西行法師

なげけとて月やはものを思はする
かこち顔なるわが涙かな

THE PRIEST SAIGYŌ

O'ERCOME with pity for this world,
  My tears obscure my sight;
I wonder, can it be the moon
  Whose melancholy light
  Has saddened me to-night?

Saigyō was a member of the Fujiwara family, an eccentric monk, and a famous poet, who lived A.D. 1115–1188. He was once in attendance on the Emperor, when a bird by fluttering its wings began scattering the blossoms of a plum tree. The Emperor directed him to drive off the bird, but the priest, with an excess of zeal, killed it by a stroke of his fan. On reaching home his wife told him that she had dreamt that she was changed into a bird and that he had struck her; and this incident made such an impression upon him, that he retired from Court, and spent the rest of his life in the church.

JAKUREN HŌSHI

Murasame no
Tsuyu mo mada hinu
Maki no ha ni
Kiri tachi-noboru
Aki no yūgure.

寂蓮法師

むらさめの露もまだひぬまきの葉に
霧たちのぼる秋の夕ぐれ

THE PRIEST JAKUREN

THE rain, which fell from passing showers,
  Like drops of dew, still lies
Upon the fir-tree needles, and
  The mists of evening rise
  Up to the autumn skies.

This verse is a good example of a picture verse, intended to call up the scene to one's imagination. Jakuren was another of the great Fujiwara clan, and lived about the end of the twelfth century.

Murasame means 'rain falling in showers, here and there', and the illustration plainly shows it raining on one side of the house only.

KWŌKA MON-IN NO BETTŌ

Naniwa e no
Ashi no karine no
Hito yo yue
Mi wo tsukushite ya
Koi wataru beki.

こうかもんいんのべっとう
皇嘉門院別当

なにはえ　あし
難波江の芦のかりねのひとよゆゑ

こ
みをつくしてや恋ひわたるべき

AN OFFICIAL OF THE DOWAGER EMPRESS KWŌKA

I'VE seen thee but a few short hours;
  As short, they seemed to me,
As bamboo reeds at Naniwa;
  But tide-stakes in the sea
  Can't gauge my love for thee.

This verse was written some time in the twelfth century; and Naniwa is the ancient name of Ōsaka.

There are several double meanings in this verse; lines 2 and 3 can mean either 'one section of a reed cut off between the joints', or 'one night's sleep as short as a reed'. In the fourth line also, *miotsukushi* means a tide-gauge, as explained in the note to verse No. 20, but the whole line, taken as printed, reads, 'How can I be already tired of thee!' The contrast here is between the length of only one section of a short reed and the long stake set up to measure the rise and fall of the tide.

The illustration seems to show the lady to whom the verse was addressed.

SHOKUSHI NAISHINNŌ

Tama no o yo
Taenaba taene
Nagaraeba
Shinoburu koto no
Yowari mo zo suru.

<ruby>式子内親王<rt>しょくしないしんのう</rt></ruby>

玉の緒よ絶なば絶えねながらへば

忍ぶることのよはりもぞする

PRINCESS SHOKUSHI

THE ailments of advancing years
  Though I should try to hide,
Some day the thread will break, the pearls
  Be scattered far and wide;
  Age cannot be defied.

The Princess was the daughter of the Emperor Goshirakawa, who reigned A.D. 1156–1158. In this short reign however, the country suffered from a very severe earthquake and a devastating civil war.

The second line is a play upon the two verbs *tae,* which are both pronounced the same, but which are written with different ideographic characters. The first couplet, taken literally, reads, 'If the string of pearls (i. e. my life) *break*, I must *bear* it.'

The illustration seems to show the Princess sitting down with a nobleman in attendance.

IMPU MON-IN NO TAIFU

Misebayana
Ojima no ama no
Sode dani mo
Nure ni zo nureshi
Iro wa kawarazu.

いんぷもんいんのたいふ
殷富門院大輔

み　　　　　　をじま　　　　　　　そで
見せばやな雄島のあまの袖だにも

ぬ　　　　ぬ　　　　いろ
濡れにぞ濡れし色はかはらず

THE CHIEF VICE-OFFICIAL IN ATTENDANCE ON THE DOWAGER EMPRESS IMPU

THE fisher's clothes, though cheap, withstand
  The drenching they receive;
But see! my floods of tears have blurred
  The colors of my sleeve,
  As for thy love I grieve.

The writer is said to have been one of the Fujiwara family, and to have died in the year 1210. Ojima is an island in the Inland Sea.

In the last line the word *iro* can mean both 'color' and 'love'; so that the meaning is, the writer's love will remain as constant as the color of the fisher's clothes, even though drenched with salt water. In connection with this word *iro*, it may be mentioned that a crimson maple leaf, when sent by a lady to her lover, is a gentle hint that she wishes to see him no more; the meaning being, that as the color (*iro*) of the leaf has changed, so her love (*iro*) has changed also.

GO-KYŌGOKU SESSHŌ SAKI NO DAIJŌDAIJIN

Kirigirisu
Naku ya shimo yo no
Samushiro ni
Koromo katashiki
Hitori kamo nen.

後京極摂政前太政大臣

きりぎりすなくや霜夜のさむしろに
衣かたしきひとりかも寝む

THE REGENT AND FORMER PRIME MINISTER GO-KYŌGOKU

I'M sleeping all alone, and hear
The crickets round my head;
So cold and frosty is the night,
That I across the bed
My koromo have spread.

This writer was another of the great Fujiwara family, and died in the year 1206.

The word *kirigirisu*, a cricket, is supposed to represent its song; the Japanese say that the chirping of crickets means cold weather.

In the picture the poet is sitting up in bed with his arm on his pillow, listening to the crickets; and in the original illustrated edition underneath the verse is drawn a cricket hiding in the grass.

NIJŌ IN NO SANUKI

Waga sode wa
Shiohi ni mienu
Oki no ishi no
Hito koso shirane
Kawaku ma mo nashi.

二条院讃岐

わが袖はしほひに見えぬ沖の石の

人こそ知らね乾くまもなし

SANUKI, IN ATTENDANCE ON THE RETIRED EMPEROR NIJŌ

MY sleeve is wet with floods of tears
  As here I sit and cry;
'Tis wetter than a low-tide rock,—
  No one, howe'er he try,
  Can find a spot that's dry!

The Lady Sanuki was one of the Minamoto family, and lived at the Court of the Emperor Nijō, who reigned A.D. 1159–1165. She was the daughter of the retired Emperor Goshirakawa, and died A.D. 1165.

KAMAKURA NO UDAIJIN

Yo no naka wa
Tsune ni moga mo na
Nagisa kogu
Ama no obune no
Tsunade kanashi mo.

かまくらのうだいじん
鎌倉右大臣

よ　なか　つね　　　　　　　　なぎさ
世の中は常にもがもな渚こぐ

をぶね　　　つなで
あまの小舟の綱手かなしも

THE MINISTER OF THE RIGHT
DISTRICT OF KAMAKURA

I LOVE to watch the fishing-boats
  Returning to the bay,
The crew, all straining at the oars,
  And coiling ropes away;
  For busy folk are they.

The name of the writer of this verse was Sanetomo
Minamato, the second son of the great General Yoritomo. He
was a famous man of letters, and was murdered in the year
1219 by his nephew, the Priest Kugyō, at the Temple of
Hachiman at Kamakura, whither he had gone to return thanks
for his promotion to a high office of state. He seems to have
had a premonition of his coming fate; for that morning, while
being dressed, he composed the farewell poem to his plum tree
given in the Introduction, and pulling out a hair he gave it to
his servant, bidding him keep it in memory of him. The assas-
sin sprang out from behind a tree, which is still pointed out to-
day, growing at the side of the temple steps, cut him down, and
ran off with the head. Kugyō was caught and executed, but the
head was never found, and so the single hair was buried in its
stead.

SANGI MASATSUNE

Miyoshino no
Yama no aki kaze
Sayo fukete
Furu sato samuku
Koromo utsu nari.

さんぎまさつね
参議雅経

よしの　やま　あきかぜ　よ　ふ
み吉野の山の秋風さ夜更けて

さむ　ころも
ふるさと寒く衣うつなり

THE PRIVY COUNCILLOR MASATSUNE

AROUND Mount Miyoshino's crest
  The autumn winds blow drear;
The villagers are beating cloth,
  Their merry din I hear,
  This night so cold and clear.

Masatsune was a son of the writer of verse No. 83; he died in the year 1221. He appears in the illustration sitting alone in his house, listening to the sound of the villagers beating the cloth to make it supple.

SAKI NO DAISŌJŌ JIYEN

Ōkenaku
Uki yo no tami ni
Ōu kana
Waga tatsu soma ni
Sumizome no sode.

<ruby>前大僧正慈円<rt>さきのだいそうじょうじえん</rt></ruby>

おほけなく憂き世の民におほふかな

わが立つ杣にすみぞめの袖

THE FORMER ARCHBISHOP JIYEN

UNFIT to rule this wicked world
  With all its pomp and pride,
I'd rather in my plain black robe
  A humble priest abide,
  Far up the mountain side.

The Archbishop was a son of the author of verse No. 76. He had just been promoted to his exalted rank, which entailed living at the Temple of Mount Hiei, near Kyōto, and this is his modest deprecatory verse on his new appointment. He is said to have put an end to his life by the method described in the note to verse No. 12

In the picture we see the Archbishop in his robes, and the great Temple of Mount Hiei, while in the distance are the wild hills where he longs to be.

NYŪDŌ SAKI NO DAIJŌDAIJIN

Hana sasou
Arashi no niwa no
Yuki narade
Furi yuku mono wa
Waga mi nari keri.

<ruby>入道前太政大臣<rt>にゅうどうさきのだいじょうだいじん</rt></ruby>

花さそふ嵐の庭の雪ならで

ふりゆくものはわが身なりけり

THE LAY-PRIEST, A FORMER PRIME MINISTER OF STATE

THIS snow is not from blossoms white
 Wind-scattered, here and there,
That whiten all my garden paths
 And leave the branches bare;
'Tis age that snows my hair!

The writer's name was Kintsune; he retired from office to enter the church, and died in the year 1244, aged seventy-six.

Note the play upon *yuki,* 'snow,' and *yuku,* the verb 'to go'; *furi yuku* means 'going to fall' (as snow), but *furi* also suggests the idea of 'growing old'. He says it is really he himself that is fading and falling, rather than the petals of his garden flowers blown by the storm.

The picture does not seem to illustrate the verse very well; it is probably meant to show Kintsune on his verandah, lamenting over his increasing years; but in the original edition, from which the pictures were taken, fallen cherry blossoms are shown underneath the verse at the bottom of the page.

GON CHŪ-NAGON SADAIYE

Konu hito wo
Matsu-ho no ura no
Yūnagi ni
Yaku ya moshio no
Mi mo kogare-tsutsu.

権中納言定家

来ぬ人をまつほの浦の夕なぎに

焼くや藻しほの身もこがれつつ

THE ASSISTANT IMPERIAL ADVISER SADAIYE

UPON the shore of Matsu-ho
For thee I pine and sigh;
Though calm and cool the evening air,
These salt-pans caked and dry
Are not more parched than I!

Sadaiye, of the Fujiwara family, was the Compiler of this Collection of verses; he was the son of Toshinari, the writer of verse No. 83, and he entered the priesthood, dying in the year 1242, at the age of eighty.

Matsu-ho is on the north coast of the Island of Awaji, in the Inland Sea; but the word also means 'a place of waiting and longing for somebody'. *Kogare* means 'scorching or evaporating' (sea-water in the saltpans), but it also has the meaning 'to long for, or to love ardently.'

The illustration shows two men carrying pails of sea-water to the salt-pans.

JŪNII IYETAKA

Kaze soyogu
Nara no ogawa no
Yūgure wa
Misogi zo natsu no
Shirushi nari keru.

従二位家隆

風そよぐならの小川の夕暮は

みそぎぞ夏のしるしなりける

THE OFFICIAL IYETAKA

THE twilight dim, the gentle breeze
    By Nara's little stream,
The splash of worshippers who wash
    Before the shrine, all seem
    A perfect summer's dream.

Iyetaka was another of the great Fujiwara family; he died in the year 1237.

The word *misogi* means the Shinto ceremony of purifying the body before worship by washing or sprinkling with water. This verse is said to have been inscribed on a screen in the apartments of the Empress at Nara.

GOTOBA IN

Hito mo oshi
Hito mo urameshi
Ajiki-naku
Yo wo omou yue ni.
Mono omou mi wa.

後鳥羽院

人もをし人もうらめしあぢきなく
世を思ふゆゑに物思ふ身は

THE RETIRED EMPEROR GOTOBA

How I regret my fallen friends
How I despise my foes!
And, tired of life, I only seek
To reach my long day's close,
And gain at last repose.

The Emperor Gotoba, or Toba II, reigned A.D. 1186–1198. He was the son of the retired Emperor Takakura, and was banished to Amagori, in the Oki Islands, where he took the name of Sen-Tei, busied himself in making swords, and died in the year 1239. He was very sensitive to noises, and it is said that the frogs of the pool of Shike-kuro have been dumb ever since the year 1200; for their croaking at night disturbed his rest, and he commanded them to be silent. It was in the eleventh year of his reign that the title of Shōgun was created and conferred upon the great General Yoritomo; which title, down to the year 1868, was borne by the real rulers of the country, the Emperor himself being not much more than a figure-head.

Notice the resemblance in sound between the first and second lines, and between the fourth and fifth lines, not fully brought out in the translation.

JUNTOKU IN

Momoshiki ya
Furuki nokiba no
Shinobu ni mo
Nao amari aru
Mukashi nari keri.

順徳院

ももしきや古き軒端のしのぶにも

なほあまりある昔なりけり

THE RETIRED EMPEROR JUNTOKU

MY ancient Palace I regret,
  Though rot attacks the eaves,
And o'er the roof the creeping vine
  Spreads out and interweaves
  Unpruned its straggling leaves.

This writer was the third son of the Emperor Gotoba, author of the previous verse; he reigned A.D. 1211–1221, and was deposed like his father, and banished to the Island of Sado. It was during his reign that the first Japanese warships were built by Sanetomo, the writer of verse No. 93, who headed a rebellion against the Emperor.

Shinobu means 'a creeping vine', but it is also the verb 'to long for'; and the verse suggests that the Emperor, while mourning over the decay of the Imperial power, still longs for the old Palace, neglected and grown over with creepers as it is.

And so the Collection ends, as it began, with two verses by Imperial poets.

INDEX

Ah! why does love distract my thoughts, 14

Ai-mite no, 43

Akenureba, 52

Aki kaze ni, 79

Aki no ta no, 1

Alas! the blush upon my cheek, 40

All red with leaves Tatsuta's stream, 17

All through the long and dreary night, 53

All through the never-ending night, 85

Although I know the gentle night, 52

Ama no hara, 7

Amatsu kaze, 12

Arashi fuku, 69

Arazaramu, 56

Ariake no, 30

Arima yama, 58

Around Mount Miyoshino's crest, 94

Asaborake, 31, 64

Asajū no, 39

As fickle as the mountain gusts, 58

Ashibiki no, 3

Au koto no, 44

Awaji shima, 78

Aware to mo, 45

INDEX

Be not displeased, but pardon me, 65
Between Awaji and the shore, 78

Chigiriki na, 42
Chigiri okishi, 75
Chi haya buru, 17

Death had no terrors, Life no joys, 50

From pain and sorrow all around, 83
Fuku kara ni, 22

Gone are my old familiar friends, 34

Hana no iro wa, 9
Hana sasou, 96
Haru no yo no, 67
Haru sugite, 2
Hisakata no, 33
Hito mo oshi, 99
Hito_wa iza, 35
Hototogisu, 81
How desolate my former life, 43
How difficult it is for men, 54
How I regret my fallen friends, 99
How sad and gloomy is the world, 82

I bring no prayers on colored silk, 24
I dare not hope my lady-love, 45.
If breezes on Inaba's peak, 16

INDEX

If I had made thy proffered arm, 67
If in this troubled world of ours, 68
If we could meet in privacy, 63
I hate the cold unfriendly moon, 30
I hear the stag's pathetic call, 5
I hear thou art as modest as, 25
I love to watch the fishing-boats, 93
Ima komu to, 21
Ima wa tada, 63
I'm sleeping all alone, and hear, 91
Inishie no, 61
In lonely solitude I dwell, 66
I started off along the shore, 4
It is a promise unfulfilled, 75
It was a white chrysanthemum, 29
I've seen thee but a few short hours, 88
I wandered forth this moonlight night, 57

Kaku to dani, 51
Kasasagi no, 6
Kaze soyogu, 98
Kaze wo itami, 48
Kimi ga tame, 15, 50
Kirigirisu, 91
Koi su tefu, 41
Kokoro-ate ni, 29
Kokoro ni mo, 68
Kono tabi wa, 24
Konu hito wo, 97
Kore ya kono, 10

INDEX

Long is the mountain pheasant's tail, 3

Meguri-aite, 57
Michinoku no, 14
Mikaki mori, 49
Mika no hara, 27
Misebayana, 90
Miyoshino no, 94
Momoshiki ya, 100
Morotomo ni, 66
Mother, for thy sake I have been, 15
Murasame no, 87
My ancient Palace I regret, 100
My broken heart I don't lament, 38
My constancy to her I love, 49
My doubt about his constancy, 80
My home is near the Capital, 8
My life is drawing to a close, 56
My little temple stands alone, 47
My sleeve is wet with floods of tears, 92

Nagakaramu, 80
Nagaraeba, 84
Nageke tote, 86
Nageki-tsutsu, 53
Na ni shi owaba, 25
Naniwa e no, 88
Naniwa gata, 19
Natsu no yo wa, 36

INDEX

O'ercome with pity for this world, 86
Ogura yama, 26
Oh! Fishers in your little boats, 11
Oh! Kwannon, Patron of this hill, 74
Oh! rippling River Izumi, 27
Ohoye yama, 60
Oh stormy winds, bring up the clouds, 12
Ōkenaku, 95
Oku yama ni, 5
Omoi-wabi, 82
Oto ni kiku, 72
Our courtship, that we tried to hide, 41
Our sleeves, all wet with tears, attest, 42
Out in the fields this autumn day, 1

Sabishisa ni, 70
See, how the wind of autumn drives, 79
Se wo hayami, 77
Shinoburedo, 40
Shira tsuyu ni, 37
Short as the joints of bamboo reeds, 19
So long and dreary is the road, 60
So thickly lies the morning mist, 64
Surely the morning moon, I thought, 31
Sumi-no-ye no, 18

Tachi wakare, 16
Tago no ura ni, 4
Takasago no, 73

INDEX

Taki no oto wa, 55

Tama no o yo, 89

Tare wo ka mo, 34

The ailments of advancing years, 89

The blossom's tint is washed away, 9

The cherry trees are blossoming, 73

The cuckoo's echo dies away, 81

The double cherry trees, which grew, 61

The fisher's clothes, though cheap, withstand, 90

The fishing-boats are tossed about, 46

The maples of Mount Ogura, 26

The Mina stream comes tumbling down, 13

The moon that shone the whole night through, 21

The mountain village solitude, 28

The mountain wind in autumn time, 22

The prospect from my cottage shows, 70

The rain, which fell from passing showers, 87

The rock divides the stream in two, 77

The sound of ripples on the shore, 72

The spring has come, and once again, 33

The spring has gone, the summer's come, 2

The storms, which round Mount Mimuro, 69

The stormy winds of yesterday, 32

The stranger who has traveled far, 10

The twilight dim, the gentle breeze, 98

The village of my youth is gone, 35

The waves that dash against the rocks, 48

This autumn night the wind blows shrill, 71

This lovely morn the dewdrops flash, 37

This night the cheerless autumn moon, 23

INDEX

This snow is not from blossoms white, 96
This waterfall's melodious voice, 55
Though love, like blisters made from leaves, 51
Time was when I despised my youth, 84
'Tis easier to hide the reeds, 39
To fall in love with womankind, 44
To-night on Sumi-no-ye beach, 18
Too long to-night you've lingered here, 62
Too short the lovely summer night, 36
Tsuki mireba, 23
Tsukuba ne no, 13

Ukari keru, 74
Unfit to rule this wicked world, 95
Upon the shore of Matsu-hō, 97
Urami wabi, 65

Wabi nureba, 20
Wata no hara, 11, 76
Waga iho wa, 8
Waga sode wa, 92
Waiting and hoping for thy step, 59
Wasuraruru, 38
Wasureji no, 54
We met but for a moment, and, 20
When on the Magpies' Bridge I see, 6
When rowing on the open sea, 76
While gazing up into the sky, 7

Yaemugura, 47

INDEX

Yama gawa ni, 32
Yama zato wa, 28
Yasurawade, 59
Yomosugara, 85
Yo no naka wa, 93
Yo no naka yo, 83
Yo wo komete, 62
Yura no to wo, 46
Yūsareba, 71